To lauren,
24/10/19,
a mic
r evl
rong
greatness is
around the
Corner

Dynamic Heights

How to Be A Confident Woman
in 7 Easy Steps

Mumba Kafula

10-10-10
Publishing

Dynamic Heights
How to Be A Confident Woman in 7 Easy Steps

www.confidentwomanin7steps.com

ISBN-13: 978-1981268559
ISBN-10: 1981268553

Published by
10-10-10 Publishing
Markham, Ontario
CANADA

Table of Contents

Foreword   v
About Mumba   vii
Dedication   ix
Thank You   xi
Introduction   xiii

Chapter 1
Step 1 – Know Your Gift   **1**
In Season   3
What is Success?   6
Moving On   10
What is Good For You?   12
Good to Share   14

Chapter 2
Step 2 – Learn How to Grow in Confidence   **17**
Confidence and Self-esteem   18
Are You Hiding Your Confidence?   19
Where Do You Use Your Confidence?   21
What is a Confident Woman?   22
Why Do You Lack Confidence?   24
Dynamic Heights C.O.N.F.I.D.E.N.C.E. Theory   25

Chapter 3
Step 3 – Know the Importance of Confidence   **29**
So You Want To Be More Confident!   32
Is Confidence a Skill, or Are You Born with It?   33
Does Confidence Have a Look?   34
How to Improve Your Confidence   35
Where Does Your Confidence Come From?   36

Why is Confidence So Important?   38
How to Build More Confidence In Your Life   40
Time to Reflect on What Needs to Change   42
How to Put Change into Action   43

Chapter 4
Step 4 – What Does Confidence Look Like?   **47**
Confidence Can Be Triggered   48
How to Understand What You Need   51
Authentic Accountable Actions   53
Three A's – Achieve Ambitious Aspirations   56
Focused Intention   57
Consistent Priority   58

Chapter 5
Step 5 – The Dynamic Heights   **61**
7 P's of Confidence   62

Chapter 6
Step 6 – Reflection Allows Confident Connection   **69**
Something New!   71
Time to Act is Now!   73
Case Study – Lisa Taylor   76

Chapter 7
Step 7 – Create Balance with Confidence   **79**
Dynamic Heights Anagrams   86
Dynamic Heights Affirmations   87

Conclusion – Next Steps   89

Foreword

When you meet someone who has made confident life changes, and has overcome life obstacles and hurdles that have led to transformation in their life, you see a renewed energy. You observe their passion and experience the courage it has taken to become more self-aware and do what it takes to succeed in their life's dreams.

Mumba is someone who has overcome life-changing events and found a way of transforming her life. When she speaks, you can sense that she has turned her life away from adverse situations, and works on getting through day by day, step by step to a better emotional state of being. You know there is something different; something resonates with you because what she is saying is true, even though you may not have heard it expressed in that way before. Her vision is a world where you achieve ambitious aspirations by understanding that you have been created with purpose, and where you are happy fulfilling that purpose and ultimately changing your ordinary life into the extraordinary.

In this book, *Dynamic Heights,* you will find themed approaches with guidelines that you can follow to empower you to transform your life, and start living the life you want to live. There are many ideas and suggestions in this book that will resonate with you. Immerse yourself into the words, delve deep, be inspired, and most of all take the steps to be the best and most confident woman you can be.

Do you truly want to learn how to be motivated and how to cultivate your confidence? After reading this book you will be inspired to lead a happier, more content, successful and fulfilling life.

Do you want to know *How to be a Confident Woman in 7 Easy Steps?* Then read on!

Raymond Aaron
New York Times Bestselling Author

About Mumba

Within this book, Mumba Kafula has shared her insights and experiences that have worked for her in her confidence journey. With this development, she has been able to empower hundreds of women to do exactly that in their own lives. She has helped them to move from their thoughts, towards action, bringing their confidence from the inside out, to the forefront of their mind, and enhancing their lives to a heightened level of strength, perseverance, and willpower, to do, as Mumba puts it, "the things they love, and love the things they do."

She has an excellent impact on women, inspiring entrepreneurs to launch their first, or revamp their existing, businesses. She brings out the indomitable strength in women that helps them flourish to be more courageous, brave and lion-hearted. Mumba is also a board member of two worthwhile organisations, and volunteers within the community whenever she can.

Overall, she empowers individuals to perform at a higher level within demanding and sometimes challenging situations, both in their personal and professional lives. Mumba embeds her core values to shine through her work, to enable her clients towards 3As—Achievement of Ambitious Aspirations—that leads to confident and *dynamic Women of Worth.*

Currently, Mumba owns and operates multiple ventures within the learning and development field, and has a portfolio of successful programmes and projects.

Dedication

I dedicate this book to my mother, Sylvia, and my son, Malachi—my true heroes—two amazing people, who have influenced and shaped my life, and who are permanently sealed in my heart forever! They may no longer be of this world, but they are always the biggest part of my world. My Mum, Sylvia, was a woman of great courage and conviction, with a heart filled with love for others, and who had a serene and a peaceful aura—a true light in my life. Malachi, my son, who came as an angel from heaven to touch my life momentarily, was a blessing of love, guidance, and angelic qualities that I will never forget—my shining star who will always be in my heart. Without you, I would not be writing this book, as out of traumatic circumstances, I was able, or provided with a supernatural ability to gather strength and determination to go on.

Thank You

Thanks, first and foremost, to the creator for giving me the words and inspiration, allowing me to discover things I would never have imagined, and helping me to find my gift. Thanks to my husband and soul mate, Bwalya, my knight in shining armour who challenges me to grow and shows me every day how much he loves and believes in me; my father, Loswell, as my great example and encourager to go on; my eldest son, Duane, for his consistent guidance, insight, and motivation that lifts me on high; and my younger son, Taye, for his encouragement, and witty, funny, inspirational comments that have kept me smiling.

Thank you to my sister, Pauline, who has always been by my side as a strong supporter, and always reminds me about all the best things about myself; and to my brother, Stan, for his advice and determined spirit, which has kept me on my toes.

Thank you Caron Gasper the person who was the first to see a book in me when I did not even see it in myself. and who planted the seed of hope: who gave me the green light to go forth and write this book, many years before it was even thought about, or came into fruition.

To all other family members, friends and clients, some of whom I have included their testimonies; in particular, Lisa Taylor, for her case study, and Cassandra Anderson-

Brown, who has been a big part of my journey, and a tower of support to me—you have all encouraged me at some point along the way—I say a big thank you, to you all!!! I truly appreciate you in my life.

Introduction

Hello, my name is Mumba Kafula, and I am a personal and professional Development Consultant. I work freelance, and my business name is Dynamic Heights. I provide confidence and motivational training, interview and presentation techniques workshops, and also one-to-one personal and professional coaching services. I have followed a path in my life that has brought me to be here today. I believe that we all have a journey in life and a road that will take us to our main destination; however, we can deviate from that road, get side tracked to another direction, take a longer route, or miss our turning altogether. I have been in many of these off-track situations in life before, but I now know I'm on the right track, my satnav is all set, and I have a planned route and a destination to where I want to go. I'm in my car, and driving, following the speed limit, and taking due care and attention to the Highway Code, feeling more confidence by the mile that my journey is leading me somewhere great.

The day of actualisation, for me, came when a meeting was held for all staff in my section of work where I was previously based. I anticipated the agenda, and was feeling quite nervous and apprehensive to what this all-important meeting was about. When the agenda item came to redundancies, I didn't feel what I thought I would feel at the prospects of leaving, or what I had thought about before, which was, "No way, not for me!" Instead, I felt a peaceful tranquillity come over me as I thought about the prospect of this major and significant life change. This sense of peace and calm, to me, was the best sign I could have to determine that this was the right move for me to take. After 21 years of working in various job roles across different departments, and taking, at one time, a part time role to start working for myself, then getting cold feet and re-entering back into full time employment, it now felt right—now was the time—now was when I had to make that life changing move.

I am happiest when I am using my qualities to benefit others. I had chosen to leave a full time paying job to realise my dreams, and start my own training and coaching business—Dynamic Heights. My eldest son, Duane, and I, spent hours and hours on the phone, talking through ideas and names that truly resonated with what I stood for and wanted to be. We both said, "YES! Got it!" at the same time, as we systematically connected on this shared vision, and came up with the name. It depicts the awesome dynamic nature within people, the heights to which my service and gift can bring them, and together, the combined greatness that is produced in them. My strap line is *3 As, Achieve your Ambitious Aspirations!!*

I have been told and I then began to recognise that I had a gift, which came naturally, and that I loved. I bring out the best in people; I help others smile when they think about themselves, and I instil pride and a sense of achievement in others. I can build people up: I encourage, motivate, and promote a more confident person, with a greater and more positive outlook to their lives.

Statements and comments like these below gave me the determination and power to carry on, and why I want to continue to help people feel good about themselves and what they have to offer, and to succeed in their careers and life expectations.

"My interview for my new job, I felt, went extremely well and I was very pleased to be offered the position. Thank you, Mumba; you are the REAL *fairy jobmother.*" – Adele Harrison

"Mumba has drastically improved my self confidence in many ways." – Matthew Myers

"I had not been confidently portraying my abilities at interviews until Mumba's intervention, and then I found my dream job." – Abigail Reid

"As a manager at the Foyer, I watched the attendees undergo a transformation and become more driven to follow their goals." – Jo Dean

"I now look forward to challenges with hope and optimism, rather than fear and negativity. Mumba's course exceeded my expectations." – Ann Barnes

"Yes, Miss Dynamic Heights lady," as I'm called by second son, Taye.

"Mum, I am so, so proud of you!" says my firstborn, Duane.

I believe we can all find our uniqueness in our lives, and follow a clear path, to a higher road in life that gives us a true sense of commitment, understanding, and purpose. Finding my purpose has been the best thing for me, and helping others to find theirs is the biggest achievement to my purpose I can make. My coaching and training style is one of care, compassion, and 100 % commitment.

The creator of life, and the universe, has laid out a road for me, which I've chosen to take; I know it is right for me, as opportunities present themselves to me, and I see it with a new and optimistic outlook that leads to many challenges, lots of victories, and increasing revelations. I'm on my journey and enjoying it with all that comes with it— good, bad, and indifferent. I want you to see Dynamic Heights as the catalyst for igniting your confidence, and for a way forward in life, for what you want and desire for yourself, which is always the starting point. Given the opportunity, this book will be the catalyst for growth in you, and provide me with an opportunity to help you *rise to shine*, and be the confident woman you have always wanted to be and find your indomitable strength that you already have within, allow me to help you bring it, draw it, or guide it out into the open and make it more visible in your life.

Chapter 1

Step 1 – Know Your Gift

I believe what we have been gifted with, our talents, our minds, and our lives are to share and help others. We all have a special gift; do you know what yours is? If not, how can you find it? And where will you look for it? Our gifts and talents come from somewhere: call it Mother Earth, Creator, ancestors, God! Whatever you believe or understand of life, be sure to know you are special and unique, and you have special and unique gifts and talents. That gift is not to be hidden on a shelf to get dusty; it is to be shining in the light, to be on show, and to keep sparkling.

In life, we all have many opportunities that come our way that we can explore and build upon. But firstly, in order to know what we have to share, we have to identify it in ourselves first, and then, appreciate it, and be willing to work on polishing it up, and providing ways to share it. When you receive a gift from someone, perhaps a friend, you appreciate that gift, and are thankful for it. That person giving it to you feels appreciated by your thankfulness, and the thought that you will make good use of it.

Your gift could be that of working with children, or the elderly, or a gift with computers or technology, a gift to sing, or teach, or speak, a gift of creativity, or a gift with numbers, being a carer for the elderly, a gift of caring for animals, a gift of organising, baking, cooking, DIY and the list goes on and on. Your gift is usually something you discover you truly enjoy or even love to do, it normally comes naturally and with little effort, people may compliment you on it, or recognise it in you as special or talented.

In the same way, the gifts and talents we have been given, need to be appreciated; and we need to recognise that when we use them wisely to benefit the lives of ourselves and others, we are also allowing the giver—be it Mother Earth, Creator, ancestors, or God—to be appreciated also. Each of us is uniquely different and, therefore, has something different to offer the world. Sharing what we have is an act of giving. Giving is loving: the more we have, the more we can give, the more we share the love.

I believe I have a gift given to me: a gift to encourage, motivate, and boost confidence; to help others to know themselves better, to work on who they need to grow into being; and to assist them to grow and nurture, and expand their talent or gift, and appreciate the special quality and uniqueness they possess.

Finding your gift can be a lifetime exploration for some. So, when you recognise it in your life, do not lose it—nurture it, and then share it.

I want to help others because, when I share my gift, it brings a greater sense of achievement and fulfilment, and I feel I'm in my truest path of existence. This truest self (I call it) resonates when you see and feel growth, change, and a heightened performance level for the better in others, which connects directly to self. You can almost see that *light bulb* moment of connectivity that illuminates in their eyes as they realise their true potential and their ability to stretch and broaden their path of confidence; and then, the drive and motivation to see it through, beginning in a journey of discovery and truth.

I have helped others to realise they can do what they couldn't do before, to gain what they have never gained, and to blossom, after being stagnated and stuck, to reach a sense of satisfaction and exhilaration. I want to help you to discover this and your own potential, to identify your gift and be inspired to share it, to grow more and more into personal achievements and recognition of what you do at your best, and in doing so, find your true purpose.

In Season

I understand confidence to be who you want to be and when you want to be it. The Oxford Dictionary definition of confidence is, *the full trust, belief, and power in the reliability of a person or thing.* A key word here for me is *Power!* There is a true sense of power in being confident— the power of self-belief. Confidence can be shaped by our experiences and be viewed differently by different people. Our confidence can be shaped through quietness, in loudness, with a fully-charged mode or a relaxed mode. Life experiences and exposure can have a profound effect on our ability to be confident in our life. Our values, beliefs, experiences and thoughts all make a contribution to our confidence as women.

Just as a flower grows within its season, I too believe that our confidence has a season. I believe we all have confidence; it's just that we sometimes have not discovered a way to bring it to the forefront of our lives. We have confidence within us, we are born with it, we have potential, and we have the ability to grow. Just like a flower with the right conditions, and in due season, our confidence can be beautiful and colourful, dynamic and different from all the other shaped flowers, and also unique, vibrant and full of the colours of life. When we have the right conditions for growth, we can shine. So, if you feel you don't have confidence, or you want more of it, you can get it. The more exposure to experiences in the areas you want to grow your confidence in, the more power you get in that area. When we combine this in an area that we are gifted in, and we share our gifts and talents, then we are truly in a place we can excel.

If you are truly looking for it, as it is something really precious you want to behold, you will find it. When we are in our true gift, we find our true confidence, and areas of our life begin to improve, towards great achievement with brilliant results. However, knowing your gift is key to this success. This knowing could take a life time to discover, but discovery is a good thing, and it is better to live and discover late than to live and not discover at all.

Confidence comes with practice, pushing past boundaries, and moving out of our comforts into the unknown.

Discovering new territory brings confidence—maybe scary but necessary. Confidence comes with a desire to grow and move past our own fears and discomfort. Sometimes our own barriers limit us, and these are the same barriers we place on ourselves.

What is holding you back? What stumbling blocks do you allow to get in your way? When you start to feel uncomfortable, what is the reason? Do you know, and can you name it? Where does it show up for you? Can you name what it is about the experience that makes you uncomfortable? Is it related to the environment you're in, the people around you, experiences from your past? Or the expectations you set for yourself, or your self-talk? Sometimes we need to ask the question in order to move forward.

If we don't know what's going on for us, how can we decide how to move forward? When you get in a car on a journey, it's always best to know your starting point and your destination; otherwise there can be many hiccups along the way.

What do you excel in, when are you most passionate, what rocks your boat, lights your fire, gives you purpose? Have a think for a moment. What comes to mind? Embrace it, and acknowledge it; don't dismiss this thought, as it comes from deep within. When we know what makes us tick, we feel confidence in this. Yes, being nervous and fearful plays a role, but we will talk about this later on in this book. Right now is to recognise it and know that it will be there. We get confidence when we are who we want to be.

There is a real sense of power when you are inside a mode of being confident. Although confidence to you may be different for me, it's all in how it makes you feel. Feelings link to our emotions, and emotions link to our actions and behaviours. Our experiences shape who we are, and our confidence can be displayed differently. We can be quiet, loud, discreet, or full on. This confidence mode can be linked to our personality and our experiences in life.

This book, *How to Be a Confident Woman in 7 Easy Steps,* will begin by assisting you to truly identify what it is that is holding you back, to help you to decide what actions to take, and to embrace your confidence from within, so you can truly let your light shine. Knowing your gift, leads to your confidence levels and your internal natural growth, coming from a place that has been destined for you—all you have to do is observe and acknowledge it, and then claim it!

What is Success?

Success and achievement are important aspects of our lives as women. I believe as human beings we are all inbuilt with a mechanism to grow, and we have a purpose in life to develop beyond where we are now. Everything that has life starts small, and we grow up; however, it comes at different rates. A bamboo seed takes 12 years to sprout through the ground and burst out of the earth; then, it takes only 7 weeks to grow to full length of up to 13 feet. At first you may think nothing is happening; for years it will look like nothing is growing, and you may want to give up, but when it sprouts, it then takes a short time to grow to full length. This reminds me of how your confidence journey can become. We can be working on our confidence for a while, and it may feel like nothing is happening for some time, but all of a sudden something happens: a situation has changed, and you have just discovered a new thought. Your thinking becomes your action; your action starts from your thoughts; you have taken a step forward. It usually appears, or you just recognise it without forcing it, then it arrives. Just like the bamboo shoot that looked like nothing was happening for some time, then all of a sudden something magical happens.

When we take small steps, or we see small stages of progress, we shouldn't give up at the planting stage; we need to water and nourish our confidence until we reap the harvest. Everything has its season, and we all have an equal share of time. We all have the bamboo potential, metaphorically speaking; however, we need to allow the time to nurture under the ground, and this hidden part is an essential component.

This hidden nurturing time for you could be in understanding yourself better, becoming aware that you do need to make changes, recognising the times when you're lacking confidence, and then recognising those times when your confidence soars.

When I work with clients, and I see growth and positive change in a person, and this comes from a clear shift in their thinking, it can be so humbling, as well as fulfilling, all rolled in one.

To pinpoint areas that need to change, they first need to be identified. It does not have to be seen as a failure if you need to make changes; it can be seen as a strength because you recognise change is needed, plus you want to do something about it. I once came across the term of what failure is. Failure = For Allowed Illusions Letting Undisclosed Reality Emerge. Which I think sums it up nicely!

I want to share some of the many testimonials I have received that help to show and identify the shift that people can make in their lives over a small period of time. Some of these testimonies are from women who have taken time out of their full day to have one-to-one coaching sessions, with a result of having excelled in mind and thought, over a short period of time. The reason I'm sharing these things with you is to demonstrate that when we focus our attention on ourselves, with an aptitude to make real improvements, we have only one direction we can go, and that is onwards and upwards. I want to use this gift I have been given to help people to, firstly, recognise that you can raise your own level of excellence, and start to work from a position beyond excellence, to a position that utilises your sense of genius—excellence in your behaviour, thoughts, actions— and in turn, this leads to a greater sense of self development and, ultimately, a more successful way to achieve your goals.

I believe we all have confidence in some way, shape, or fashion within us, although we can't be fully confident in all areas in all times. We have specific areas of our life that we feel much more confident in than in others. Think about your life and an area in which you feel confident. What is it that makes you feel this way? Have you done it before? Is it familiar to you? Is it something that comes naturally or easy to you, and almost effortless? Is it something you have had to practice and become better at over time? If it is an area of life you are working on or need to improve, or a friendship, a new relationship or a clearer purpose—whatever your area of confidence—take a few moments to think about what it took to get it. When we have confidence in an area, and we understand the process or principle as to how we got there, we can then transfer this into other areas we are less confident in. Using the same tools, process, or principles, we can adopt or align it towards this new area of focus. We all have the capacity to change. Confidence can be a journey and can come over time, with patience and dedication. Our inner self can gather momentum over time to be more confident in a new skill, or character change, or approach or attitude; this will instil an inner sense of esteem that leads to something powerful.

When we practice, as the saying goes, practice makes perfect. It is not that we are looking for perfection here but, in some way, confidence is perfecting our way of being that helps us to shine forward and feel good about ourselves.

These words sum up how we feel within relation to being confident in a certain area: we have full trust in ourselves; we have a sense of power in relation to how we feel and in how we apply the situation or context; we believe in ourselves and the action or ability. This is true confidence when it resonates with us, and we feel it in our whole being.

Look at what it took to make you feel confident in a given area of your life. When we give value to the steps and stages we have gone through, and the ability to overcome hurdles, trials and challenges, and can see that we have come out on the other side, we begin to feel and embrace a true confidence that feels, looks, and even tastes great. We all have a genius within. Let's now start to look at how we can tap into our greatness and really begin to shine.

Moving On

To develop your confidence, there has to be an element of preparation and practice on the levels of change that will be able to support you going forward. I have created a series of workshops, webinars and online programmes that will help support you on your journey to self-discovery. This book is an opportunity to provide insight, ignite your awareness and, potentially, stimulate your understanding around what you might need to change, as well as how you can do it, while providing a clearer direction on how to obtain it. These support packages can enhance and develop you further to increase and develop your skill set in order to manage more affectively your confident approaches.

Do you want to take that next step in a practical and purposeful way? Then connect with the Dynamic Heights website, or visit the free bonus site on the front of this cover for further updates and information available to you. If you want to gain confidence at a faster pace, and build your personality at the same time, this is an important step to take on your journey. If this sounds like something you are interested in, then at the end of this book, you will find information and further details on how you can access my programmes, and truly begin to rise to shine. This can be a great way to work for you, either on your own time or with a package of support, or with the option of working one-to-one during a confidence coaching programme that will support you on a more in-depth way.

When we decide to do something that will improve us as a person and help us to feel better about ourselves, this will move you into a heightened level of personal development and achievement. This can bring excitement, but at the same time, it can also bring a fear within.

Why do we get fearful around areas of potential growth or change? This can be due to the unknown, a lack of direction, being unsure of what will change or how it will impact you, not believing you can do it, or a host of different reasons. However, in the same vein, in an excited mode, you have a rush of adrenaline that provides butterflies in your stomach and a heightened sense of anticipation. You're holding your breath at the prospects of what could be. These mixed feelings of fear and euphoria are normal, and that's when you do need to go for it—this is the body's way of preparing us to do something very different and unusual to your system. This complexity of emotions is linked to the igniting of deep connection within and endless possibilities, which can come from your new leap of faith, into the entity of the unknown, into renewed confidence. This fear and excitement is linked so closely to your divine purpose, and that is why the emotions are strong as you begin to connect with a source of power that has a real and tangible hold on you, and which has the potential to change you forever. So, if you're feeling this now, then do not hold back. Go for it. Connect with Dynamic Heights right now! Do not wait for those feelings to be quenched or reasoned out, or put away for another day, now is the time for you to shine.

What is Good For You?

Do you believe you can have confidence in the areas you want it in? Do you believe it? Well, I am telling you that you can have it, if you really want it. Like most things, we repeat or practice; we work on, we hone in on, and get it, eventually. Just like confidence, it is a skill, and a skill is a learnt behaviour. Every skill we have ever known, we have learnt. So, why not learn a new skill of being confident. You already have confidence within, waiting to be ignited, so building your skill set in this area will provide an opportunity for you to connect your skill with your already inbuilt confidence that needs nurturing in order to come out.

However, what tends to happen is that most of us have an inherent ability to disconnect with what is good for us because what is good for us usually takes more effort, energy, and refocus, and that can be like hard work. Or maybe it could be we want something for nothing! Everything in life we want to improve on, we must act on it. Without action, most things just stay the same—stagnant and untouched and undeveloped. We do not get a true reflection of a powerful result when we do not put our true energy and thrust into something we want in our lives. If we really get determined, focused, and committed, we can eventually get to our destination; it's just a matter of time.

It will take courage, long-term commitment, and much patience. It may not be overnight, and it may take time to grow. Like a flower, it blossoms from a seed; however, it needs water, sunshine and soil to truly develop. Our confidence can be much like a flower. It can be embedded deep as a seed into the earth's soil, similar to it being within us; it needs water, and this can symbolise as our desire to change. Then it needs sunshine, which can be our practice and ongoing trials of defeat we sometimes face. Then, eventually, it flowers, blossoms and blooms, and that's us in our full confidence, shining bright and beautiful. Do you want to be in season and flowering in true bloom? Then read on!

What are the things we strive for or want in our lives? Are they based on immediate reality or are they futuristic dreams? How many of your dreams have come true? If we look back into our lives at a time where we truly desired something, looking back, can you say you got it? If so, how did it materialise? Usually, it came about by effort, or valuable intervention on yours or someone else's behalf. If it hasn't arrived yet—this dream of yours—do you know where on the receiving spectrum you are on your journey of discovery towards your dream? On a scale of 1–10, do you really believe that you deserve it? If it is high on this scale, more than likely you are doing something to determine it coming in to your path. If it is low on the scale, perhaps it is not as important as you think, or your self-esteem can be low, and you may feel unworthy of receiving it.

In life, we can choose to focus on the important or the non-important things. When you are working in line with your values, desires, and dreams, this leads to a more focused energy alignment towards your end goals. How much, on the scale of 1–10, is being confident important to you? Understand why it is important to you, and then work out what you need to do to place a higher level of importance and value in your life towards achieving it. We can have most things we put our minds to, but it takes real effort and sustained action in a consistent way. Do you feel you could try harder? What changes will you make to improve obtaining your confident life in a much easier and quicker way?

Good to Share

I'm wanting to share fundamental insights that I have found, obtained, created, observed and, most of all, valued in my life. I feel it is our responsibility to share the great things of whom we are, with others. When we appreciate something about ourselves, then we should know that that is a greatness within our lives, worthy of recognition. We should appreciate, embrace and acknowledge our gifts, our experience's, our talents and our strengths. I write this book to share what I have with others: the stages of confidence that helped me, and others, whom I coach. Sharing what I have means I'm not wasting it; I'm utilising it by sharing it with as many people as I can.

If you have something good to share, don't keep it to yourself—shout it out! Serve others with your divine gift, and share all of what you have with others. Whether you have an inner urge to do something that links with your passion, that you excel in, of which someone has given you great feedback, or it's one of your greatest strengths, does it come effortlessly to you, almost like doing it with your eyes closed? When you love what you do and could keep on doing it, more than likely you are in your gift—in your highest place of being and doing what you have been created to do, at this time, in this place, in this way, in your way!

I believe we all have a higher calling deep within, and a connection to the Creator of life and this world. Whether we see it, feel it, or recognise it, I believe a force connection is always there, and whether we choose to ignore it or acknowledge it, is another matter. However, it comes to us, we must embrace it and treasure it. If we see it as a treasure, we will look after it. We can share that treasure, not keep it within—share it and make the world a happier and better place.

I believe, when we share a part of ourselves—our higher being, for the good of others—I imagine we release almost something like a metamorphosis response within us, and in turn it replenishes with a greater scale than we originally had within us.

This is my theory on the scale of giving for the good of others: it provides a reciprocal effect almost simultaneously. On our journey of giving and sharing our gift, we can do this in many ways. I choose to do so via Dynamic Heights: to create a dynamic impact, from a great height, in the lives of those I have the privilege to touch as I connect within the coaching or training services Dynamic Heights provides. I write to share the hidden treasures within me, and to assist you to find those hidden treasures from within you too.

Chapter 2

Step 2 – Learn How to Grow in Confidence

Why do women need to be confident? We need confidence because confidence is part of our nature. To have belief and self-esteem in who we are in this world requires a level of confidence in what we bring to it, and what we bring is life; we bring goodness and we bring light into the world just by our nature of being a woman. We have inbuilt connections to our Mother Earth, like no other creation or being on this planet.

We, as women, have been created with uniqueness: we are intuitive; we are amazing nurturers; we have great abilities and talents; we are good supporters of others; and we can meet so many needs. We are honoured in society, and society would not exist without us. Of course, we did not create all this ourselves; we have been gifted with this inbuilt natural nature that we need to truly value. However, to allow this true manifestation to emerge and grow in our lives, we have to acknowledge it comes with a sense of confidence in who we are and of knowing our capabilities, and it also comes with responsibility to be the women we are destined to be.

Seeking and believing in the opportunities that come our way to assist us in bringing it to the forefront of our insight, intellect and intuition: To do this, there is a need to acknowledge our need to constantly grow in being confident in whom we really are and what capabilities we have been given.

Confidence and Self-esteem

We feel self-confident when we trust ourselves to be able to perform a certain task or action. To perform, even when the task is new, different or difficult, it's stepping forward with a sense of trust that can make all the difference to the outcome. This can lead to a feeling of bringing forth a powerful, double dynamic of stepping into who you are as well as stepping into the unknown.

This duo of states can support your ability in raising your performance level to a higher level. This repeated action leads to optimum manifestation of being in your best state of being, confident in who you are and whom you have been created to be. We also need to be able to respect our self-esteem and the power behind it to give out what we have.

We need to believe in our own ability, creating our value within us that reflects in a favourable opinion of ourselves that is not limiting us in any way but elevates the good in who we are. When we have a realistic impression of ourselves that exudes from us, we then have full regard for what we have to offer, and full regard for who we are, confident in whom we have become.

Having self-efficacy refers to a level of inward trust and belief in our capability to carry out a certain task or attainment, which supports your confidence in a way that provides motivation. Having self-esteem, self- efficacy and self- confidence links to how we feel, think and behave. It all links to our cognitive, physical and emotive processes. Through belief and trust in our lives, brings a higher proportion for our life, and our motivation to bring forth new areas of growth.

Are You Hiding Your Confidence?

What have you learnt recently that makes you more aware of something that you were unaware of before? That's exactly what confidence is: a learnt behaviour built on the power that you already have within you, just like learning a new skill! When we want something we don't have, we can go out there and get it! Perhaps a fear grips you when you want to do something different or something bold. Perhaps you lack the ability right now to bring it out, because you are unaware of how to do it. If you have an ability to learn a new skill, then you also can be as confident as you want to be in that new skill.

As our confidence comes from our desire, which is within us, and our new behaviour of being confident can be learnt, we can, therefore, learn to be more confident and bring it forth into our own being. Learning to be more confident, with a desire to be more confident, with the added power of existing confidence that you already have within you, then it is only a matter of time and nurturing that your confidence will grow. To be good at any new skill, it takes practice, and practice, and more practice. Your skill in confidence can grow through your own nurturing and putting yourself more in situations where you can apply confidence—how you handle these new confident changes is up to you.

When I first became a personal development trainer, I had the qualification but not the experience. I always used to refer to my notes and training plan, checking and then rechecking—am I on the right page I need to be on; have I covered all the points I had planned; was I in the right time allowance for the topic; am I running over; have I covered everything? —and so on, and so on, almost in rote fashion. I dreaded questions, as I was sceptical of my abilities and, although I was wanting to give a good answer, I was not sure of my own ability to respond, and felt intimidated in high numbers of learners—sometimes up to 30 at a time. I feared losing control, feared being misunderstood, and lacked confidence in meeting their needs. That was then, in my early days of learning to grow in my confidence in a new skill area, using the confidence I had within, and nurturing it with time and practice.

Now, many training sessions later, I am glancing periodically at my notes or plan. I go with the flow and energy of the group, and apply the training accordingly that may require slight flexibility or switching the order of the plan, in my time allocations. I am open to adaptability to enhance the learning and the experience of the learners. I have lots more confidence in my ability because I have had much more practice, and I value the inner confidence that has been nurtured and valued from within me. I don't wait for questions anymore; I ask them. I enjoy answering them and discussing my field of work. Now, classes of 30 plus, with mixed ages, cultures, abilities and experiences, do not phase me. Yes, there is a slight element of nerves to begin with, which is understandable in new situations, but in time, I adapt, connect, and unwind into my confidence and my flow. I am not as phased as I used to be, even with mixed abilities, ages, and life experiences. I can multi task and plan and structure the delivery in a systematic and orderly way, use my training plans to accompany me and adapt when especially there are on-the-spot changes needed from time to time, but my true confidence is able to shine.

Where Do You Use Your Confidence?

My point is this: all the capacity to manage this situation, was already within me. It was only time, experience, learnt behaviour, and practice that allowed it to be brought out. If I had been daunted and put off my initial experience, and had decided to give up, I would never have experienced the true potential I have for this kind of work. If I had not continued through any fear or anxiety I may have had, I would never have experienced the buzz of the many dynamics which have been taking shape within me during this time in my life.

I discovered that truly making a difference in a positive way in the lives of others builds my confidence in who I am and what I have to offer the world. I learnt that if we hide or shy away from our potential and true confidence that comes from within, we give away opportunities to grow, we limit our capacity to shine, and we reduce our ability to develop and bring forth those hidden talents, strengths, and gifts that we are so unconsciously longing to bring forth into existence. There is a saying: use it or lose it! This is so true in that our abilities can be lost; they can just pass us by and slip away, or lie dormant and not be discovered. When we plough on through and learn to rekindle, reignite and keep the fire burning, we can uphold and bring forth a renewed dimension and direction in our lives, which can truly change your life forever! How can you find it if you do not know where to look or what to do?

When I say look within, think of your past achievements, successes, and highs; what are you most proud of? What skills have you used or are still using, and what skills have you forgotten you had? What have you lost that you can find, what makes you smile, what are you passionate about? Asking yourself questions is a good start. What changes would you like to see in a new life, a new beginning, a new day? Where do you want to see your confidence grow? Why is this important to you? Wait and expect the answer, as it will come, but be ready to listen and acknowledge it when it does. The answers are within you! In the morning, ask your question, and wait with expectation—it will come.

What is a Confident Woman?

My definition of a confident woman is one who is true to herself, who recognises her gift and wants to share it with others, even as far as sharing it with the world. A confident woman is one who is not afraid to start all over again when she messes up or makes a bad move, or makes a mistake or regrets a decision. A confident woman is one who is able to triumph through hurt, heartache, despair and pain. A confident woman knows what she wants and takes steps to get there.

A confident woman is one who sees victory and hope, and has faith and trust in the unknown. A confident woman works on being all that she wants to be, now and for the future. A confident woman does not give up when people mistreat her, abuse her, take from her, look down on her, or bring problems her way. A confident woman stands up for justice, and pain and neglect of herself or others; she looks for purpose and good, and can self-sacrifice for the benefit of others. A confident woman has integrity in what she does and in her beliefs, and doesn't need to copy or stand on others toes to get what she wants. A confident woman is authentic and real, and has nothing to prove to look or feel good—she has her own security in her own ability. A confident woman doesn't falter if others speak ill of her or try to discredit her worth. A confident woman knows when to move on or away from those who intend harm or show her distrust, or lack standards of credibility or integrity. A confident woman is a woman of worth, who knows her values and stands by it.

Do you recognise yourself? I'm sure you can, if you look deep enough. It will, in most parts, resonate with you some aspects of who this confident woman is, and maybe even working on some parts too, you may connect with some, if not all, of who she is. We have it when we need it—when we have to rely on self, with conviction for doing what feels right to us at the time. Go for what you believe in, especially if it feels right for you and its coming from a good place. Don't feel guilty when you give to self and recognise it is your time for receiving something good, remember if you have no time for valuing you, you will have nothing of worth left to give.

Why Do You Lack Confidence?

We lack confidence because we doubt, fear, and have no focus. We doubt success; we are fearful of what we cannot see, and we are not clear at what we want to be focused on. When we have no belief or power or trust in ourselves, we don't hold enough potential to move forward. We have pockets of it at times, and we have surges of it on occasions, but if we don't truly have a goal to work on, in a consistent, systematic way, then we lack substance. Are you consciously aware of your confidence developing, or is it something you stumble across or realise after the fact? When you consciously direct your confidence, and channel it in a focused way, you can use your mind to refocus your energy and power towards what you want, and directly away from what you lack.

We sometimes think we are in lack because we do not have everything we what or need; but because of our limiting beliefs or value we place on ourselves, we miss out, or take what we have for granted, or don't value what we have, or do, or who we are, enough to recognise that we already have it. For example, there is the mum who manages so many things around the family and home. She believes she has no ability to work out finances, although she does it every day while juggling spending across the household. Or, she thinks that she cannot do a high demanding job because she lacks skills, but all the time, she is a multi-tasker and a great organiser and a methodical thinker and she is good at administrating areas of responsibility; she is a good timekeeper, collecting kids and dropping off from school; and she is creative with food preparation and meal times, etc., etc. We have it but don't recognise or value it.

We are good or great at some things but not so great at others. What it takes for us to be confident in one area can be taken or transferred into the less confident areas we hold in our lives. What we need to do is find out in which areas we are truly confident in and can thrive in. When we find out what that is, we can name it and know it, feel it and recognise it, and own it and be able to apply it. Then, and only then, do we have the required ingredients to apply it to another given situation we want to be confident in. It's all in the recognition of the process used: the stages, the actions, the beliefs, and the motivations that are taken. I call this theory the *Dynamic Confident Theory*.

Dynamic Heights C.O.N.F.I.D.E.N.C.E. Theory

With the Dynamic Confidence Theory, you have a:

Can do approach to life! and, where your mind goes, your energy flows.

Openness to new possibilities and opportunities! that come your way; however, you're ready for them and see them when they arrive.

Now is the time! not yesterday or tomorrow: be in the now, and embrace the present, not the past, which has gone, or the future that has not arrived yet.

Find your true self! who are you? What makes you, you? Your personality, your character—what is it about you that is special?

Include others! in your goals and your dreams. Nothing on earth can be done successfully without the recognition of others in our lives; we need support, help, and guidance—we can't do it alone. Who are they for you? Acknowledge them.

Dynamic you! Where is your dynamism? Can you find it? We are all dynamic in our own way. Be aware of the height of your achievements in life.

Every day is a new day! And a day of new beginnings, being grateful and joyful for every new day.

Never give up! keep moving towards your goal, and you will get closer and closer to it.

Connect! what you do well into other areas of your life. Understand what it took to get you there, and reapply it elsewhere—the process and approach can be emulated.

Expect good news! and always be positive and faithful that your dreams can come true.

The Dynamic Confidence Theory provides an opportunity to apply a strategy in life that works, and relies not always on self but also on a greater sense of a power beyond our own understanding, which works with us as we confidently strive to apply ourselves in a better way in this world. With continued knowledge and repetition, being aware and being hopeful can assist a new way of living and building a sustained, positive approach to life. What we have done well, we can duplicate into other aspects of our lives. What we need to do is understand what it is that we do well, and how, and then use the same approach to the rest of the areas you want to improve on.

Chapter 3

Step 3 – Know the Importance of Confidence

In this short exercise, you will be able to rate yourself and see the results. It would be useful to complete this before moving on, as this will help give you a more realistic and balanced perspective, on a clearer confidence level. Please be honest: the best way is to write down your first thought; don't tick the box you would like to be in; just tick the box that represents you as you are now.

How important is it to you to be confident in most areas of your life?

A. Very important ( )
B. Little importance ( )
C. Neither is or isn't ( )

In which situation do you feel more confident?

A. When I'm around people I am fully familiar with ( )
B. When about to face a familiar situation ( )
C. When I am well prepared ( )

When are you least confident?

A. When going into a new situation   ( )
B. Meeting people for the first time   ( )
C. When I have to do something I am unsure of   ( )

How much do you want to be more confident?

A. Desperately   ( )
B. Not at all bothered   ( )
C. In some areas but not all   ( )

Are you a completer/finisher?

A. Yes always   ( )
B. Not always   ( )
C. Only sometimes   ( )

Are you currently working on being confident?

A. Yes   ( )
B. No   ( )
C. Only sometimes   ( )

Do you believe you can be more confident in the future?

A. Yes definitely	( )
B. Not quite sure	( )
C. No I do not	( )

Now, score yourself: read the corresponding areas where you ticked mostly A's, B's, or C's, This will give you a greater sense of focus for your confidence, and will also give you an idea if you need to work on any areas for improvement, going forward.

Mostly A's: You seem to be trying hard at your confidence, perhaps you could relax more and allow it to flow more naturally. You may be more prone to manipulate a situation, because of your need to demonstrate your ability to succeed, when, possibly, you hold many doubts internally but tend not to show it or ask for help. You may tend to spend little or no time on improvements to yourself personally because your focus is more on other people. You may tend to compare your worth to others. It may be useful to try and see how you can become more grounded in your own positive opinion of yourself, rather than allowing your thoughts to dwell on what you think others are thinking.

Mostly B's: You are working towards improving your confidence. This may take some more effort or determination, to move on quicker than you are. You may sometimes find it difficult to stay on course, and can sway or change your mind quickly. You can be easily distracted or feel overwhelmed by the many changes that sometimes need to be made. Try aiming to sustain a 48-hour confidence stance, regardless of the situation, and then assess how much impact this focused 48-hours can have on you. Staying on course can take time to build in momentum.

Mostly C's: You seem to be lacking in areas of confidence. This may be affecting you more, as it shows up more often in a visible way to you. It may be something you think about a lot. You may come across a lot of opportunities to grow, but you tend to let them pass you by most of the time, as you can tell yourself it's not the right time–but there may never be the right time! It may be that your thinking may need to change more to the concept of *the time is now!!* By waiting for the right moment, and putting things off for the future, that moment may never come or may pass you by.

So You Want To Be More Confident!

Why do some people seem to appear more confident than others? What makes them stand out from the rest? Those who are not feeling confident in areas of their life may ask themselves this question. The answers they come up with may help them! Or it may not!

I believe, to recognise the internal strengths we have, and then to value them, is one way to uphold your confidence. Drawing upon them, pulling them to the service of our minds, is important. When we identify, give value to, and embrace our experiences, skills, and abilities, then we automatically feel more worthy; this worthiness will undoubtedly lead to an added confidence in who we are, and in our capabilities.

Perhaps being more confident lies in recognising the patterns of our behaviour within certain circumstances. The reason I say *certain circumstances* is because not all of us lack confidence in the same areas. Some are more confident in one area than others. We all have differing experiences and challenges, and sometimes these experiences can lead to a belief about ourselves that may not necessarily be true. Or a belief about others that we make up in our own minds with no true evidence.

Identify which areas you have confidence in, and understand the reasons behind that situation, and why the confidence is there. Now, compare it to a situation you are not confident in, and see what is lacking. Then, you can identify how you can transfer the experience of being confident into the experience of being unconfident. How did you get to this point of confidence? Is it familiarity of the experience? Or is it a learnt behaviour? Or both?

Is Confidence a Skill, or Are You Born with It?

If we lack value in who we are, we lack esteem. When we lack esteem, we lack confidence. When we lack confidence, it hinders our true potential and, ultimately, our futures lives.

By nature, as a creation, we are generally positive people; we do, however, need to tap into our inner gifts more frequently, to see this positivity shine. When we are in a good circumstance, it can have a good effect on our attitude to life; however, when in a bad circumstance, it can have a negative effect. Can our confidence be determined by our circumstances? Only if we allow it to be.

Does Confidence Have a Look?

Confidence can look different to different people. Most barriers in our confidence are internal and are triggered by our beliefs; however, we can get external barriers that appear by something or someone else. Identifying our internal and external barriers helps us understand if it is something we can work on in ourselves, or something that relates externally; in which case, we need to work on how to overcome it. Neither is as simple as it sounds: it takes determination to make real and lasting change. In order to work on any barrier, we need to identify it and acknowledge it. Once we acknowledge that we have a barrier, we can then work on reducing the barrier. To work on reducing anything, we need to take action. The quicker we act, the sooner we can get to our end goal.

Being positive about yourself is a strong survival technique. When we feel low, our confidence takes a knock, and this makes it hard to feel good about ourselves or our situation. Without confidence and a positive self-image, it's even harder to take the steps needed that may help you turn the situation around.

Getting a grip on life brings new and daunting situations, so being as prepared as you can to handle difficult situations is very important. This will mean recognising and valuing strengths and qualities. Sometimes it may even mean changing the way you think about yourself.

The more optimistic we are, the better our performance, the clearer our thinking. This comes from research. There is a definite link between optimism and performance! Therefore, it is more an attitude that is required to break free. Being confident is more about having a set of skills and learnt behaviours creating a positive look.

"Whether you think you can or you can't, you're probably right." – Henry Ford

How to Improve Your Confidence

Remind yourself that confidence is linked to fear, and fear is a feeling, and not always rational. Then, facing your fear is –easier said than done!! Facing a fear takes strength and courage, which we all have deep within us. How we use it, pull it out and present it, can be a staged approach. Acknowledging that you do want to do something about it is the first step. Identifying what will make you feel more confident in that situation will determine which part of the barrier you will need to work on first. What will you achieve if you work through this and overcome it? It is always useful to know this, as it can heighten the determination to succeed. Set yourself 3 m's: miniature, mediocre, and massive goals to achieve. Start off small, and then move to mediocre; this will give strength, insight, and courage, and it will help you to know how to deal with the massive. You will feel more motivated once you face it, and more confident once you are motivated.

There's nothing more powerful than knowing someone else has done what you so badly want to do. Recognising that it can be done. Seek people who have fought and overcome their own hurdles; hear their stories, or what they can share as insight. Find books to read of authors who can help your journey.

Often, when we face hurdles, we feel defeated and want to give up. If you remind yourself, at these times, that every little success involves many challenges, then you will suddenly see that your current challenge, once overcome, can be turned around and seen as, in fact, a sign of progress.

Where Does Your Confidence Come From?

I believe that all confidence comes directly from within. Within you there is a desire for your confidence to grow. This desire usually is linked to the desire to be successful, to be able to have satisfaction and fulfilment in your life. To have this sense of achievement usually has to come with an ability to be able to complete certain actions, or the understanding or awareness that you do not have the ability to complete a certain action. Whichever it is, all these inbuilt natural desires we perceive are fuelled by having a certain level of confidence to attract it, or to work on having that desire in your life in the first place. So, these desires do come from a natural place from within, whether we choose to recognise it as such or not.

When we experience something, it manifests a feeling, good or bad; this then leads to an acknowledgment of the feeling, and then we can choose to appreciate it or not. To be able to choose to appreciate something in our lives, we need to have a certain level of understanding of what we appreciate about that particular given situation. Because we are human, and prone to inconsistencies in our life, in our thoughts and our actions, we sometimes can lose who we are and what we have the potential to do or be. This feeling of lack, or reduced states of mind, limits your ability to be consistent in your approach towards success, and then becomes accepting in, or of, the circumstance. Our recognition of being confident in these states of mind becomes limiting, and this then turns up as vibrational entity within our thoughts.

So, when we do not recognise, due to a lack of inconsistent presence of your success or achievement, fulfilment or satisfaction, we get a knock-on effect in our confidence. This reduces our ability to regain, recharge, and reconnect. Our recognition of our success is vital to our ongoing growth in confidence levels. Through recognition, it means we have had this heightened state of mind at some point in our existence.

It is never lost; it just lies dormant until we can revive and energise it again. So, with limitations of consistent thought or experiences, we get the notion that we do not have confidence, or our level of confidence is low. So, to reignite our state of mind, and give value to what we have, we need to build our confidence muscles by reflection and recognition of our past experiences, achievements and success.

Why Is Confidence So Important?

When we have confidence, it leads to inner calm and a good sense of awareness about ourselves. Having a good sense of self is about knowing what makes you tick! We will not know everything about ourselves; we will have blind spots too, which others see, but we don't see. We are not superhuman, but we will know the areas about ourselves that are important to us, and we usually will know the areas of life that we need to change. The things we want more of in our lives, we know we have to work harder for. You may not have it all, but you are confident in what is missing, and usually have some notion as to how best to get it. When we have true confidence, it is linked to how we feel about ourselves and our self-esteem. I say *true* because I believe there is such a thing as false confidence. This is where we externally show that we are confident by how we carry ourselves across to others; but, internally, we feel it very much as lacking. Inside out confidence, is important, as it is manifested more in how you feel about yourself, how you carry yourself and, more importantly, how you think about yourself—and that reflects on how you come across to others.

Why is confidence so important? It is important in knowing who you are, and feeling good about it too. Confidence is not just an outward appearance; it is also an emotional, internal attribute that comes hand in hand with the outer perspective, in terms of what people see. Dynamic Heights sees confidence as an essential and important element to prospering in life. It provides a sense of achievement, trust, and belief in yourself. It builds on recognising that confidence stems from within. It starts on the inside, and builds, with time, energy, and familiarity, on the outside. It is important because it portrays you, the real you, in a positive light; it provides an assurance of an "I can do" attitude.

Being able to reflect on self is important too. Your confidence journey must utilise reflection, as it's a means to help you to identify with your true self. When we reflect, we become more self-aware. When we are self-aware, we can have opened eyes to see what we may need to change. When we can see what it is we need to change, then we can think about, and act upon, the improvements we need to make with concrete efforts to change. It is through initial reflections that we become clearer in how to do this. So, make time to reflect, and make time to change from those areas of reflection you know you need to improve.

Through reflection, we can develop a more heightened sense of being, and be taken more seriously when we are presenting in a confident way to the outside world. Although confidence is not about showing it to the outside world, it is about having a full sense of that moment, in a positive light, that feels good and responsive to the circumstance you are in; it's a natural sense of being that feels good and feels right. This can only come in time.

Make a confident stance today if this is not you, and build on the importance of having true confidence in your life, through reflection and timely changes, so that you may progress on to the bigger things that the future holds for you.

How to Build More Confidence In Your Life

Putting yourself into situations that push you into new territory is one way to build your confidence: those areas of your life you would prefer to steer clear from because it raises anxiety or increases your stress levels, where you feel lacking in confidence to take on. These will be the areas that will improve your confidence most, and at a quicker pace, as long as the area is a healthy choice that links with improved well-being and a safe environment. However, it comes with challenges. When you move ahead in these situations, it often becomes a confidence booster. When we go beyond our comfort zone and make attempts towards doing something new or different, it focuses our minds on new things.

This focus may bring situations we want to improve on to the forefront of our minds and, therefore, our conscious minds too. When we become more conscious of something, it draws our self-awareness more to it. This can ignite our energy flow towards it. It can then boost our momentum to further in this area, like a cycle effect. This can be a relief towards movement you have put off for a long time, and to know you finally have done it! This will lead to a sense of satisfaction, achievement, and accomplishment, which will positively impact on your well-being and mind-set.

If you can change the way you think about something, you can literally change your life. Our thinking is usually where most of our self-belief and self-doubt come from. Take incremental steps or giant leaps—whatever works for you, and will impact you one way or the other, but make that start. Once that feeling is achieved, you want more of those feelings, and confidence can become addictive; you strive towards it more and more, once you have had it—that *feel good factor* sensation kicks in.

Recognise the things that you are confident in, be aware of it, and embrace and acknowledge it.

Know the things you want to grow in; then work on it slowly or fast paced—you choose.

Use the principles laid out in this book to monitor and see how you're doing, or what needs to change.

Focus more on success, optimism, and positivity around those chosen areas; watch for what's happening too.

Trust yourself, and keep trying; don't give up too quickly—persevere.

Be willing to learn, to see things through fresh eyes, and embrace change; don't resist it, embrace it.

Time to Reflect on What Needs to Change

Sometimes we can be oblivious, or block out or refuse to see what needs to change in our lives. Yet sometimes we know exactly what needs to change. But that doesn't mean it comes easily. It can be a long, hard process over time. The biggest bonus we have towards change is, awareness; this is the best place to make that start. From awareness can come acceptance that you, and only you, can make that shift. From acceptance, you can move into reflection, reflecting on specific aspects of your life where change is required. From reflection, you can move into documentation. Document, and take notes physically; write or type what is required to change, and note it down in the present tense—not from the past with what you should have done, or the future with what you want to do—but write it down as if it is happening right now!! Write the things you want, as if you are already experiencing it, feeling it, seeing it, and living it!

When we reflect, we look back, and this is important: to see from our past what we need to learn, change, or keep the same. Looking back is one way to assess how your confidence has changed, or what you want to focus differently on. Being reflective is a good thing, as it allows you a good chance to see what works, and to draw on those past skill sets you forgot about, or which have been lying dormant. You see more of the things that have been beneficial or rewarding and useful to your progression. Then, you are in a better place to work on the *how*, and in a better place to do it *now*. The *how* takes you to a real place to begin working: working on your actions and methods of approach and technique, to follow and enable you to thrive; focusing your energy on the outcome, and what it will look like, how it will feel and sound, and even taste like! How would I think, behave, and feel if I had this particular thing in my life? These feelings, or sensations or thoughts, are those that can be the driving force towards getting you there right now.

Reflection is good; however, it is even better when you adapt, change, and improve from your reflective moments.

How to Put Change into Action

To change anything, you do need to be realistic! This is important so that you do not take on too much, or feel overwhelmed or powerless to change. This can easily happen with the best will in the world, so begin by choosing an area that will make the most difference to your life, and then map out small stages that you can do to make lasting change happen.

You can maintain this staged change by choice. Choose to sustain it over a period of 7 days to begin with. If you can make 7 days in a change of anything, you are on your way to truly accepting that the change is possible and can be manifested in your life. Like anything, repetition is a good, practical way to keep things going. With repetition comes action, which over time this repetitive action can be embedded within your subconscious mind.

Once you are subconsciously connected, it will become easier to draw upon that knowledge to effect change in future similar situations or experiences. There will be some familiarity in your mind of the change, and this will draw upon your subconscious to trigger a similar response. Then it's up to you to act accordingly from that choice of response triggered.

At this triggered stage, however, it can be possible to digress back to the original default mode of doing things. So a quick responsive decision to act when triggered, which will be linked to an intuitive subconscious connection, is what is required at this stage of change. Not dwelling on a deeper contemplation towards actions, as this could lead you to reverting to the go-to mode of operating or responding to a given situation or experience.

When we arrive at a given situation or experience that we have a choice to act on, it is at that very point where our will power comes into play. There is also the measurement of the actual desire: perhaps we could view it by asking, on a scale of 1–10, how important is it to you, or how much of a desire it is to you? where 1 is least likely, and 10 is most likely a yes.

Willpower and the scale of desire to change are two areas that can alter or stop any commitment to change. Depending on what score rate each has at any given time. This point of knowing can only come at the point which it is required to be shown through the manifestation of that desire. Choosing to act on it or not comes at the exact point of change, because prior to that, it is only a thought of what you want to do or desire to do. Only at the time where you make the decision, your scale of desire kicks in. You could rate your scale from 1–10. If it is at the lower end of the scale, you may become weak-willed, or have a reduction in that will and desire. If it is higher up the scale then there will be a strong will and a high desire to see and maintain the change.

Dynamic Heights Change equation:

Choice of action + high willpower x high desire = real change.

Chapter 4

Step 4 – What Does Confidence Look Like?

What does confidence look like to you? Have a think for a moment. When you think of a confident person, what do you see? What do you hear, or how does it make you feel? Does confidence even have a look? What words would you use to describe a confident person? Perhaps bold, focused, charismatic, articulate, engaging, friendly, sociable, energised, determined, winner, know what they want, say what they mean, a clear sense of direction, comfortable in their own skin, got it together?

Do any of these statements describe you? Can you connect with some but not all? Would you like to be more like this? Whatever it is, or however you connect, confidence can be different things to different people, and can fluctuate depending on circumstances and experiences. Many aspects of our developed confidence can come from experience, repetition, and practice. It is not always a natural skill to all people. Like anything you get good at, patience, determination and, of course, diligence (one of my favourite words) helps.

When did you last describe yourself with some of the above descriptions? When can you say you last came across in this way to yourself also to others? Is it something that comes naturally, or do you have to work on it? Either way, confidence looks a certain way and means a certain thing to you—only you know how it feels to you.

It can also be asked is confidence a skill that can be learnt. Or is it an attitude we acquire to use? Is it an approach that we take? A mind-set we have? How does it come about? Or can it be an element of these? Yes, it can include some or all of these elements. So, if you have them, is that all you need to be truly confident in yourself? Does it have to be felt by you, or does it have to be recognised by others to be true confidence?

I believe true confidence is knowing in yourself you are confident in a certain area; it does not have to be acknowledged, validated, or confirmed by someone else, although this is an additional confirmation. It can simply be a feeling of confidence that comes from within—a feeling that exudes powerful trust and reliability in yourself or the particular act you are undertaking. Confidence can be whatever it looks like and however it feels to you! And simply nothing more than that! Let's look at some of the components that can help build your confident muscles towards a stronger, confident ability to perform.

Confidence Can Be Triggered

Triggered by Skill – All skills are learnt. This means, if you want a skill you don't have now, you have the capability to learn it. Being confident can be considered a skill; therefore, it can be learnt. The thing with confidence is, it must be repeated, and repeated often, to do it well. It's like the theory of *unconscious incompetence,* where you are unaware that you need to change, or *conscious incompetence*, where you are aware you are working on the change but have not fully grasped it yet. *Conscious competence* is when you're picking up an ability of the new skill, until it can be done in an *unconscious competence* rote fashion without thinking, and, is when you are in the skill learnt phase, towards developing a confident competence.

Triggered by Attitude – An attitude is a point of view or inclination towards something or someone, and then your approach reflects this in your manner, behaviour or speech. We can have a confident attitude that is received by one of these mediums, and can show a confident attitude towards something or someone. If we can determine our attitude and inclination, then we can determine the same with our confidence, if we are so inclined to do so.

Triggered by Approach – Our approach is usually linked to our experiences and our stance on a situation. When we approach something full on with intensity and commitment, we usually get something done well. If our approach is half hearted and lacks focus, the result will not be as successful or a fulfilling one.

Triggered by Feeling – Our feelings can impact our confidence, as our actions relate strongly to how we feel. Our feelings relate strongly to how we think; therefore, if we think confidence, we can feel it more within us, which will impact our actions. If we hone in on how we feel in each situation, it will be a good way to keep a check on our emotions and actions, and not go overboard.

Triggered by Mind-set – Our way of thinking, or our mind thoughts, can be the determining factor linked to all our attitudes approaches and feelings towards our situation. We can have negative or positive mind-sets, which can impact us in different ways. Our minds are powerful, and we determine what we want to place in it—to our benefit or to our detriment.

Triggered by Perspective – We can have a certain perspective or view point on a given situation, depending on how we see something. This perspective could change for many reasons. Perspective gives us different ways to view a situation, from different angles. Our minds can be influenced by people, situations, or words—indeed, we can however influence our own minds, it's all about perspective.

Triggered by Words – Our words can help us to feel more confident, just by how we say something. We may not feel it, but somehow, we can allow our words to impact us subconsciously without even knowing it. There is an enormous power in our words; that's why affirmations really can work for people, as we can believe them into our subconscious brains. The key is retaining it, and recalling it as it's quite easy to forget.

Triggered by Thoughts – Our thoughts influence us every day, in areas of our confidence. Our thoughts come in and out of our minds daily, and they will fluctuate daily, hourly, and by the minute—a lot of our thoughts are just that! A thought: not particularly real or evidence based but mostly just purely a thought. It can lead us to make choices around being happy or sad, mad or glad. Because our thoughts come in many disguises and shapes, we need to be aware what is working best. We can have control over our thoughts, with practice; therefore, our level of belief in our confidence starts with recognising what our thoughts are saying about us.

How to Understand What You Need

If you identify there is a skill set you want to have that you do not have, then make a point to work on it. As skills are learnable, the first stage is to identify what you want it for. For example, if you want to learn more social media skills, get more active in this area. There is nothing like practical action to learn something new. Spend some time exploring, asking questions, and seeking answers, and try out new things.

As women, we sometimes want to get everything just right before we try something out when, in fact, the growing is in the trying, most of the time: actually, clicking into a new programme on your computer and seeing what happens, typing a note or writing something, and sending it. Look around at different media sites and check-out what is happening—take that step. Over time, steps can become big jumps forward.

Familiarise yourself, and be in the picture by taking part. Incremental steps make change happen. Let go, step-by-step, of what is controlling you from being able to move forward.

When you know what you need and have worked-out what it takes to get it, then the next stage is action to complete the skill set required. Your needs can change just like your circumstances. Sometimes we actually think it is a need when, in fact, it is basically a desire or something we want. A need is essential as a requirement and a necessity; not being able to get it could be detrimental. However, when we are confident in areas of our life, it becomes more essential to separate our needs from our wants, and our must haves from our desires. For example, in order to get your next job, you may need to research the company and revise your CV to be prepared. Now, you may say "I need" a new jacket for the interview to look my best, but it's not quite a need or an essential to getting the job—there is a difference.

Needing to do your research and prepare for the interview is a much bigger need. Wearing a new jacket is not going to get you the job. It may help you to feel better in something new, or help you to look smart but, essentially, on its own, it is not going to do it! Yes, you may have two areas of focus, but one is more necessary than the other. There is a difference. If your energy flows more to looking the part rather than being the part, you spend your time looking for that perfect jacket rather than working on your interview preparation. When this happens, your *want* supersedes your *need*, and you jeopardise opportunities to be a quality candidate. Separating your *want* from your *need* allows you to focus confidently on those things that are more meaningful to who you are, and your end goal and ultimately a priority focused, quality of life.

Authentic Accountable Actions

When we decide to take action, we then should be able to carry it out. So, how can we ensure we do that? By having someone who is going to hold us accountable to what we say we are going to do. This is partly important to assist you to move on: having someone who can check-up on you and see how you're getting on. A coach or a mentor, or a friend, could be just the right approach to take, to see you from one situation to an improved situation. When you have made an accountable action, then you become more authentic, as your accountability kicks in when carrying it out.

Being authentic is being true to self, and true to your desires and your dreams. If your focus is to please someone else, to do something more for their satisfaction than for your own—although helping others is fine— if done consistently, you lose the essence of who you really are, and your authentic value diminishes.

While it is important not to be selfish (and sometimes selfless acts are necessary), if your soul purpose is for the benefit of other people's desires, and does not include your own, this can be soul destroying, and does not allow you to truly live your authentic purpose in life.

When we are more authentic and true to ourselves, then our gifts, manifest themselves in our life. We can tap into our own inbuilt drive and passion that guides and sustains us, with our desired goals. This happens because we are in line with our purpose, and we do not become weary when we are following, and are connected to, our gift; and we understand that, at the right time, if we don't give up, we will discover new oceans and new beginnings.

Our gifts are divinely given, and each of us has our own unique amount that is provided to us in just the right proportion, in a very unique way. My gift will not look like your gift, or anyone else's for that matter.

Just like our finger prints are unique, and so are we, and so is our gift. We have been provided with a divine gift that is presented in our lives, which we can choose to honour or choose not to tap into. It is divine because it is of a spiritually connected source that is beyond our own understanding. Some relate this divinity to many different things, but I relate it to God.

I believe there is a God, and his purpose for our lives is divinely given and is unique and purposeful for the benefit of ourselves, as well as for the benefit of others. When we embrace, accept, and are utilising this gift, then our fulfilment starts to ooze out, and we become more aligned to our path or destiny.

Not finding our gift, denying its power, or having it but not using it can be a waste of a gift. So, I believe, as well as to live life and live it to the fullest, and in recognition of respect for life, part of our purpose is to know the God who gave us our gift and aim to understand how we can more effectively use it. Part of our knowing our gift or talent is to do the best with it with all our ability when we discover it. Don't leave it a life time to discover your gift. Find out what it is, and don't underestimate small gifts as insignificant, most precious things can come in small packages.

Most of the time our gift can come from something we do quite naturally, or it could be something you discover you really enjoy, or it could be something someone tells you that you are good at and you realise you have a talent in that area. You may have more than one gift!

Yes, this will take work; yes, this will mean action; yes, this will take time; however, the rewards far outweigh the works. We have a lifetime to find it, so the sooner we pursue it, the easier it can become for us: When we use our gift, and the more we understand it, we will know how it works in our favour, and then we have longer to use it in our lifetime. As a sense of fulfilment, it is an incredible feeling; it links to our authentic integrity, and aligns with our purpose.

I believe my gift is to help others find their gift. I believe my gift, which I can sometimes, in business, refer to as my unique selling point, is helping women to realise and find their indomitable spirit that lies within them, and help them not only to realise it but to also continue to draw it out. Writing this book is sharing my insights and my own gift, and highlighting a divine wisdom that flows within me, which can never fade unless I allow it to or it is taken away. I have channelled and used my discovered gift through

Dynamic Heights Training and Coaching Company, and my Thoughts To Action Membership Club, where women are flourishing in their gifts, and getting to know more of who they can and will become.

3 A's – Achieve Ambitious Aspirations

3 A's is a core theme throughout the service of Dynamic Heights. The focus is on achievement in confidence; when you have an ambition to do something with an aspirational entity, then your confidence can soar like an eagle spreading its wings as it flies across the sky. Our aspirations in life lead us to be more ambitious, and our ambitions in life lead us to be in a place to achieve them. What are your ambitions and aspirations in life? No matter how big or small you may think they are, the process to achieving them confidently is always the same.

Action is power, and your powerful actions provide you with the ability to enact the 3A's. Think about where you would like to be in three, six, or twelve months from now. Do you feel, right now, you have an ambition in life to aspire to? What would it look like, feel like, sound like? What importance can you allow it to have in your life? If it is important, what steps could you take to get you there? Each step, with determined action, can take you one step closer to your dream. You can Achieve a focused Aspirational and Ambitious life.

Focused Intention

When I was working in a full-time job, I knew, deep-down, that I had the potential to do something new, something different, and something dynamic. However, I struggled to realise that what I was thinking and yearning for was a new direction in life. I didn't find out what it was or even give my thoughts a name. I didn't know what it was—disillusionment, discouragement, yearning—and no attached name not at all.

Thoughts came and went; inspired feelings came and went; desires came, and desires went. Deep-down though, the feeling to express differently, to do differently, was always there; however, I suppose I did not allow my thoughts to go deeper into what it was I really wanted to become. Could it have been a subconscious fear of the unknown?

Circumstances and times do make a difference, and the timing of my circumstances was not allowing the breakthrough to take place. My confidence level was limited by the unknown, the unsure, and the untested! Therefore, I did nothing! When I eventually came to a place where I gave my desire more focused and intentional thought, when I prioritised time and energy to thinking with depth and more recognition, then, and only then, did my desire start to come alive. My confidence towards myself grew, and the faith I had in myself increased, and my knowledge, coupled with the power of prayer, increased greatly.

Consistent Priority

Then, as in my introduction, came my day of actualisation. What then channelled my ability to move from working full time to going self-employed, was consistent priority. From a deep sense of peace with the new thought and new perceived direction, came a realisation that this feeling had to be right—such calm and tranquillity.

My thoughts became more consistent, and focus allowed me to see potential and possibility. This, then, assisted my confidence to explore more, and widen the possibilities. These explorations then ignited my inner being and aligned with my core truth. I believe I became alive to who I was to become, and with this, an automatic aligned confidence to that truth was born. I believe I had something that we all have. I then knew I had OCD—Options, Choices, and Decisions to make—not obsessive-compulsive disorder, as the anagram is usually referred to as, but options to choose from, choices to make and, from those choices, decisions to take.

I believe our confidence increases when we are truly aligned with our truth and our core purpose. Our lives spring into action and our actions become driven with purpose, passion, and potential. Looking back, I can see the pattern and the direction, and I am so pleased, and truly grateful to the creator of life for helping me to be in a place of realisation, where I feel truly aligned with my passion. I allowed myself to move into the unknown, and this has allowed me to realise what my potential, for my life and for my truth, can really become. I can grow into and find more hidden treasures of myself. I shudder at the thought of constant new beginnings, of depth of life, and an abundance of favour towards me, as I delve into action towards real growth and change.

As I'm writing right now, I'm stopped by a phone call from a coaching client, who I have provided interview coaching to a week previously. She called to tell me she got the job! After a full, updated conversation over the telephone, Feeling honoured that I was one of the first people she called, that she valued my support and wanted to share the good news. I sat back with a real sense of satisfaction and achievement in knowing I'm in the right place, doing the right things. I know this because these areas of focus and support for others I have in my life, my work, and my business are having a real and lasting impact on individual lives!! Gifts are meant to be shared, and if you can get paid for it at the same time, that's truly a bonus!!

Chapter 5

Step 5 – The Dynamic Heights

7 P's of Confidence

Power – Our power comes from within, and we need to recognise it. A lot of the time, we see power as something that others own, something bigger or in more authority than us, but power does not always need to be big and bold and outwardly displayed. Our power can be internally led, quietly confident, and integrally placed to shine when required: power to say, power to do, power to be, power to be you. When we can authentically be who we REALLY are in life, this is when we have true power: a power that is alive and not hidden; a power that allows your true self to come out; a power that trusts self and your own abilities, not relying on others approval; valuing it but not being reliant. Your confidence shows a sense of power, and this confidence needs to be powerful for you. It is not what others determine power to be. It does not have to be as the world sees it—as status, income, or material possessions—power, to me, is simply just to *be*.

Performance – To be able to perform well, you need to utilise your knowledge in an effective way in addressing the performance level required in any given situation.

Performance, the second P of the seven P's, usually has the connection with doing something well, and doing something right. The dictionary definition of performance is *the action or process of performing a task*, which means it needs to be seen to the very end in order to be complete. Words that tend to link, or go hand in hand, with the word *performance,* are production, show, or presentation; all these words require a person to be available in that moment, and taking action to carry out the task successfully.

Most performances have degrees or levels from a low to a high (e.g. a high-performance car is of a higher standard that a lower performance car. There is less power and stamina in the low performing car.). So, to be of high performance, it takes high performing tools and abilities. This is exactly how our confidence grows. Any one of us can have low graded confidence or high graded confidence; it's all about levels of intended action and levels of consistent performance, over time, and over long or short spans of application. So, to be of an optimum level in our confidence, it will take time, practice, commitment, and preparation.

When we feel good about our performance we feel great so, to feel good it is worth working on the high-performance level in whatever we want to perform in. To perform well in your confidence means to be moved up to a higher level of performance, and to feel powered up while doing so.

Patience – When we have the capacity to be tolerant in and around problems or circumstances, and to accept situations when we are not happy about them, without getting anxious or annoyed, but have restraint then this is commendable. Patience is not easy; it is not normally a natural quality of a lot of people. Some are better than others at being patient, which usually requires elements of humility, to rise above a situation and allow your thoughts, your actions, and your words to not only demonstrate for the good of one (usually is yourself, by the way) but to be considerate for the good of many.

If you think you have a lot of patience, then think again! When did a situation last not go your way? What was your thought, action, or spoken word, or did you hold it in and become resentful? Being patient usually has setback or suffering involved. However, with perseverance, there usually comes some kind of reward or compensation over time, although not always at that time when we feel we most want it.

Learning to be more patient enhances your confidence as you are growing from the inside out; and any positive growth, particularly inbuilt and character forming, is good— positive growth is necessary to improve your confidence. So, essentially, it all has a lasting impact on boosting your confidence. Starting strong and staying strong, in anything, takes persistence, as well as determination, which I think comes hand-in-hand. Staying on track with something, consistently takes committed energy and focus; being determined to see something through to the end is paramount when it comes to being patient.

One of my most favourite words I really like to emulate—even the sound of the letters intrigues me—is the word *diligent.* It takes a certain sense of diligence to persist with anything. It is taking diligence to complete this book, and let my thoughts, understanding, knowledge, experience, and desires to be transformed onto the pages, and to see it through with all the challenges and setbacks along the way, coupled with hope and anticipation—and, of course, with patience—right through to the very end. With purpose, diligence, and desire, you now have my book in your hands.

Persistence – Being a confident woman, in 7 easy steps, encapsulates the application of the 7 P's, to allow flow and ease to take shape. You will have to embrace being persistent because you won't always feel confident in all situations; you will in some, more than others. However, being persistent through those times of feeling less confident will be a good thing in the long run, as pushing past any barrier will always produce effective results, particularly resilience.

You will not always want to be in situations where you are having to push and step beyond your comfort zone; when you build your confidence in one area, you then master it with persistence, and then you generally gravitate towards finding another opportunity to focus your energy towards some other area of life you now need to master with confidence. Being persistent in building, sustaining, and growing along your confidence journey will take persistent actions, with diligent steps.

Positivity – How you view or how you want to see something can be from a negative or positive, pessimistic or optimistic, standpoint. We all have, as I call it, OCD— Options, Choices, and Decisions we can take. When we acknowledge and accept that a positive mind-set brings about positive physical and psychological impact on our human bodies, then how we apply positivity to our day, week, month, and year should have a more aligned, positive embrace. It is also beneficial to know it is a fact that positivity improves heart rates, and decreases stress levels. You have more focus, and a clearer, generally all-round good persona when in a positive state.

A more effective level of concentration, is maximised and improved when we stay positive. When we have options to choose from, positive or negative, and when we have choices to make about our options, and we make a decision, the rest is up to us. When we look at putting situations into perspective, we should always be ready to see the positive aspects that enable us to have a clear assessment on what may need to change or be improved on. I always say that the positive will always outweigh any negative.

Potential – To have potential means there is a possibility to do more: more than you have already achieved; more than you do right now; and more than you can possibly hope or imagine. More than you will ever know, there is capability in potential, and there is unknown territory in potential—an existence yet to be discovered and yet to be achieved. We all have potential, but not all of us achieve its true worth and value to our lives. We squander time, skills, and money, and reduce our potential from moving and striving closer to our goals, dreams, and, ultimately, our true destiny. It's a form of self-sabotage, without consciously knowing it.

When I think about the word, *potential*, I also keep thinking about value: the value we place on ourselves. When we feel worthy of something, we value ourselves in that worth. When we feel accepted for who we are, and have a sense of self-respect, we feel justified in that respect for ourselves. When we value ourselves, it upholds our worthiness and esteem, and we are then in a better place to recognise, appreciate, and discover our true potential.

Like a hidden gem buried in lots of sand, we may take a good while to discover it; but when we do, it gives such a fulfilling sense of joy, that the searching and the time it took to find the gem becomes well worth it. What is your true potential? To find it, we have to stretch ourselves. Search, stretch, look, hunt, and explore, with a deep sense of anticipation and expectation, and you will find it.

Prayer – There is power in prayer! I believe this because of my experiences of prayer to the Creator of life. There is a meaning beyond our imagination and understanding that ensures we can communicate with the omnipotent source of life! This is something phenomenal: an existence that has an immense powerful energy. How much of a privilege is it for us to have such a connection?

When we communicate with the Creator of life, it is a two-way process, like a relationship; and if we pray, we can also listen, watch, and learn from our lives, we get responses back. Your ability to bond with the Creator, is available to you. To have a true relationship, the communication line of prayer has to be established. What an immense privilege to have access to all that you can ever hope, dream, or imagine—we can pray for it or pray about it.

Answered prayers come in many forms—sometimes as *yes*; sometimes as *no*; sometimes as *not yet!* —if we have a faithful trust, not only in what we do know but also in allowing the unknown to take shape in our lives. A confident, faithful prayer of hope brings forth a power of love on another scale to our lives. If we open our eyes and look around us—I mean, really look and take all of life into perspective—we can begin to appreciate the world in a way that channels us towards wanting to know more about our maker of heaven and earth. Bringing forth a supernatural power that we can tap into, if we open our eyes to see and feel and take it all in. Our God confidence will flourish, like a flower blossoming and unfolding into a new, brighter, clearer, and fresher perspective. Prayer has the power to change, and even the power to help with building your confidence. If you have not already, why not try it!

Chapter 6

Step 6 – Reflection Allows Confident Connection

Do you really want to develop your confidence and move your journey forward? Remember, as women, we have gifts, and we all need confidence to bring it out! We have, so far, looked at where our confidence comes from, what confidence actually looks like, and why it's important to grow our confidence, as well as connecting with the 7 P's of confidence. It is now the time for you to reflect on your learning and shaping towards your confidence goal. Are you at the right place to move confidently into your power? Power referred to here is being in the presence of all that is waiting for you.

How confident do you want to be?

For what reason do you want to be more confident?

How will it benefit you and your life?

These questions are important to answer, and only you can answer them. When you do answer them, and know why you want to walk into your gift and your power, and truly own it, then your reflections will become deeper, and more meaningful and productive to the change you need to make and want to see.

Take some time right now to stop and reflect on any changed thinking since reading this book. Notice any shifts in thought, behaviours, and approaches that you have taken or are considering taking. You need to understand this one point during your reflective moments, and if there is only one thing you get from reading this book, then make it this:

Our changes in confidence are incremental and difficult to see unless you are looking for it, or unless you reflect well. It is slight, and it comes in short bursts; with tiny steps and small changes, it grows at a rate that is subtle, and can almost be deceptive. Watch, listen, feel, and learn in your growth. Don't dismiss your new-found confidence as a blip, or a coincidence, or just a temporary moment of courage. No, it's none of those; it is the true *you*—you are blossoming and growing, like a butterfly opening its wings right before your very own eyes.

Now, reflect, ponder, embrace, and acknowledge your new-found strength, your power, and your glory. Reflection is important: it gives you a starting place and a perspective on things. It allows you to connect in with your feelings. It's about serious thought or consideration to something. So, if you have not started yet, then why not do so now...

STOP, REFLECT, CONNECT—RIGHT HERE, RIGHT NOW! Before moving on!!!

Something New!

To return to something mentioned earlier regarding learnt skills, when we start something new, we operate within an experience of *unconscious incompetence*. In psychology terms, there are 4 stages of competence, often known as the competence learning model, by William Howell. We start off not aware of our incompetence, or that we are in an incompetent state of being. Then, we can become aware of our state. Just like driving a car for the first time, we become conscious of our incompetence— *conscious incompetence*. After some time of practicing driving, we become more conscious of our competence, so we are in a state of *conscious competence* as we begin to improve our awareness of our improvement, and it becomes stronger. We become better off, and stronger in our convictions and our ability. We continue till we pass our test and start to drive well, and after driving for some time, we become *unconsciously competent*, where our actions are automatic and natural, and within a subconscious state. This is exactly how our confidence develops: in stages— stage by stage, practice by practice. Notice and embrace it. This is one way to become more confident. Another way is to gather and obtain support along your journey, where you enlist the support of another to assist you through the stages.

One such support can be through a coach or an accountability group, or via workshops or training sessions, or online courses or webinars. If this is one area you would like to utilise rather than working on your own, then part of this next section of the book will introduce you to how you can obtain this from Dynamic Heights Training and Coaching Services. Although there may be other additional services you may want to explore for your own growth needs, you will, while looking, know what feels or looks right for you. One size does not fit all! However, if what I've been saying to you on these pages, so far, resonates, connects, and moves you in a forward-thinking way, and moves you towards a new direction of action, then maybe these next stages or exploration of how I can help, support, and work with you, may be what you need to tap into right now for your journey to start or to continue.

Available to you are tools, techniques, practices, one-to-one support, group accountability membership, training and workshops, online courses and webinars—including this book! If you're feeling a spark of excitement, of being lifted, with eyes widening at the opportunity to glow, then this is for you—don't deny, put it off, or give up now!

I have developed ways to build you from unconscious incompetence to unconscious competence, through my tried and tested approaches. If you have had an *aha* moment—a *light bulb* moment—while reading this book, then don't be surprised; it is your inner self talking to you, and all you have to do is take the *action*!

Check out www.dynamicheights.com, and www.confident womanin7steps.com, for more information on sign ups, registrations, appointment bookings, and workshop dates.

Time to Act is Now!

Whether it's a silent whisper, a strong calling, or a recurrent thought, listen to it, and move with it. When we have consistent thoughts about something that will impact us in a positive way, but we don't take action, we sometimes rob ourselves of our own development, and lose out. As the saying goes, *if you don't use it, you lose it.* It could be a lack of motivation to start something new or do something different. To get motivated, you need to do something different. To be motivated, it takes action. A good word, to put before *motivation,* is the word, *self.* It's not what others can do for you; it's what you can do for yourself. If you have a passion for change, or to do something different or great, enthusiasm and positivity helps in a big way towards self-motivation. Building motivation habits is something we could all improve on. We can set goals that motivate us to make change. We can make small changes, but the key is to keep moving, to not give up, and to not doubt.

We can learn so much about ourselves when we work on breaking bad habits, and improving on good ones. When we push past our comfort zones, we understand more about what makes us tick. Be persistent and don't give up! Persevere and keep building on what is good. Be patient, as good things will come to those who wait. Know your skill sets, your talents, your strengths, and your passions. Hold on to your values, and keep your integrity. Seek opportunities, and be ready to claim them when they arrive. Be alert and be watchful, and don't be distracted or too negatively influenced; keep positive, encouraging people in your life, and do things that will make a good difference.

Remember, you have a power in you that is unique and different to anyone else. This power can be truly ignited through prayer. Even if you are sceptical, or doubt some of this, is it not worth a try to see if there is hidden potential awaiting you?

Being confident can apply to any aspect of our lives; it's up to you to make that decision to start. Start anywhere; start somewhere; just start! Like any journey, it starts with that first step. And that first step starts with a decision to change, to do something different, and to get a different result from what you are used to getting. As the saying goes, if you keep doing the same thing, you will get the same results. So do something different!

I hear the testimonies and feedback from women, on their confidence journey, whom I work with through my gift to help them find theirs: their confidence levels increase; their hope and optimism increases; and their ambitions and aspirations are being achieved. It's amazing for me to hear and see this transformational change and incredible impact, and almost unbelievable, if I was not witness to it.

This is not bragging; this is not being deluded; this is not boasting; this is not pride: this is a sheer demonstration of recognising what I have, and using it to benefit and allow women to recognise, through my *tapped-into USP* (Unique Selling Point), how I help them to draw out their *indomitable spirit* from within them. It's incredible and beyond my explanation.

If I don't share it, I'm holding back on what I know to be true. Even writing this book, it's not my natural tendency to shout out or talk about myself, except when needed in regards through pursuing my work areas, and usually only for the benefit of putting a point across or providing an example. I recognise that holding back and keeping quiet, and not allowing my expression to reach, touch, and change lives, is doing the giver of my gift a dis-service, and holding a selfish and ungrateful attitude.

So, I push past my fears, I push out of my comfort zone, I make a start, and I do it for the best of reasons, with the right intentions, and with my own integrity. I know it's the right thing, and I am doing right by myself. Even if this book only touches the heart of one or two individuals, then I've done what I've needed to do. If it touches more, then I've magnified the impact, and I'm very proud of that.

Gaining feedback from clients impacts me to know I'm on the right track, going the right way. It empowers me to know I can make a difference, and it releases my insecurities and strengthens my faith in the bigger agenda of touching people in a way that supports their life.

Each one-teach-one, is a saying of old. I want to pass it on, so they can pass on what they have. I want to continue to be blown away from their experiences of growth, and I never want to take what I have for granted. I always want to grow in my strength and resilience, through times of good in my life, times of bad, and times of pain. I know that there is a greater power operating beyond my control, and I would rather be walking and working within it than be walking or running away from it. Wouldn't you, too? Read the following case study to help illustrate the impact of how I feel when real change takes place.

Case Study – Lisa Taylor

Lisa arrived on day one of the Women of Worth Training and Coaching programme, for confidence and motivation, and personal development in business. She felt low in her self-esteem, and apprehensive about who she would meet and how much better they would be than herself! The push to get through the first day was an enormous one, coming from a place of feeling rejected in her emotions and thoughts. As Lisa tried to explain to me how she was not feeling so great that morning, and how she had struggled to get there, I saw the tears appear and slowly roll down her cheeks—silent tears, flowing along an angelic-like face.

All I could see was a woman with so much courage, going through so much pain, but still carrying on through the adversity, and arriving—shakily, but arriving nonetheless! Having used all her reserves to get there, she seemed to have no more energy or capacity to get past the arrival stage. Due to her frail disposition, I excused myself from the group, and asked Lisa to accompany me to the kitchen for a coffee. There, she explained further her plight, her dismay, her anguish, and her pain. Staying professional, authentic, and empathetic, I provided comforting words of encouragement, expressing how far she had come, how much of a safe environment she was in, and being just where she needed to be, just at the right time. I explained that she was with women who are used to tears being shed, and who have an abundance flowing of resilience and stamina, and that lots of things happen for a reason we only later in life start to fathom. I told her that she was appreciated as a member of the group and we all wanted her to stay, to embrace the comrade of women ready for purpose, coming together with a mission and a focus in mind.

"If the tears need to flow, let them flow; come out of the room, and come back any time," I reassured her, "but don't go home. Better to cry here than at home alone." I assured her, by the end of the day, she would be dry-eyed and connected to the group in a way no one would be able to explain.

Tears in her coffee was the morning, but connection, focus, energy, and woman power was her medicine by the afternoon. Lisa stayed and took in all that was meant for her that day. Being there was all she needed—being still and embracing the moment. Tears and pain changed to laughter and joy. She received a change of emotions that day in an immeasurable way, which sustained her and took her to another place of being a Woman of Worth—worthy of friendships, worthy of joy, worthy of peace, worthy of letting go!

At the end of the day, I reminded Lisa of a message I got at a time I was very low, from a complete stranger who came towards me with the words that have resonated with me, even up to this day. She said, "Remember, sunshine *always* comes after rain."

Lisa went on to say in her own words:

"I feel a difference and a shift in my life; this course has truly transformed my life. I have recently completed the Women of Worth programme, with Mumba, through her Dynamic Heights company. I started the course, feeling incredibly vulnerable, lacking in confidence, and being tearful, and I certainly didn't feel like a Woman of Worth. Mumba encouraged me to stay for the first session, which I did, and I can honestly say it's been the best decision I've ever made. The past 8 weeks have been truly transformational in my life, to the point where I am talking about plans to open up my own business. Mumba is an absolutely lovely lady, who also offers ongoing membership support, through her company, to women who want to continue to stretch and grow. It's been invaluable; thank you for all your support."

Chapter 7

Step 7 – Create Balance with Confidence

Transformation is truly a great thing: to see change right before your eyes; to see someone shift in their thinking, in their mind-set, and in their actions; to see a change for the good; and to see actions that are made not just from your emotions but also from utilising a clear thought process—one of protection; one of goodness; one of hope! Lisa is one case study, in one life that has been changed, and her life will be different going forward, no matter what. Yes, ups and downs will come, and yes, it's true: life happens. Just because we have a set-back doesn't mean we won't be able to come back! However, once transformation has risen, it's only time and concentrated application that allows it to truly shine forth into your life. Once released, it will emerge again, and again, and again. When we change for the good, something inside is released, and we can never be the same!

We all have a gift. Discover your gift, and don't allow opportunities to pass you by without grasping and connecting with it, utilising and embracing it, as a part of your life. If you go through all your life not recognising it, then that can be soul-destroying. Be aware of what your gift is. It may not come to you over night, but you can bet it will arrive at some point within your lifetime. Be ready to accept and embrace it. No matter how small or large you perceive it, it is still a gift. Sometimes great things come in small packages. There is one message of truth I really want you to grasp from reading this book that is this: Make time in your life to discover your true value and your true worth.

You are a dynamic woman, full of worth. Discovering and owning this worth, in my eyes, is the real and meaningful essence of success in life. Success, to me, is not what you can get, or how you can get it; it's about what you can give! When you use your free gift to give to others, and value, respect, and honour yourself along the way, you will naturally *receive*—as a consequence—you don't have to look; it will flow into your life like serendipity.

Transforming and shaping in your gift of giving to others lives will no doubt be embedded within a love for others, and then, and only then, can we spread the rewards of true success. If you can utilise your gift, and make a living out of doing what you love, then so be it. That could be seen as a double dose of satisfaction. This may not be for everyone, but it will resonate with some of you. When you have a passion and desire to share your gift, you may want to utilise it in a fuller capacity within your life, and shower your gift on a regular basis. Of course, because it is freely given, it does not mean you cannot utilise it to serve your own personal daily needs, as in food, shelter, and warmth. This must be looked at if you are going to sustain it on a more full-time basis, as it is all right to gain an income in doing what you love for the good of others.

There may be those who do not want to develop it full time but want to use it sparingly amongst those they choose to use it with, and this, too, is fine. As long as you use it and don't lose it!! Whatever or however this looks, feels, or is for you, it's okay. Create and balance your life with your gift, with true confidence, and with a sense of fulfilment— and only you know what that is, how it feels, and what it looks like for you!

I believe we are all on this earth for a purpose, and that purpose is to discover our purpose. I understand we have a Creator of our lives that gives us more than we could ever hope or imagine, but it is up to us to discover it and, once discovered, not to hide it, not to put it under a table, hidden, but to place it on top, like you would a lamp, to shine bright, and brighten your whole life, like a flower blossoming in the sun, to grow and to truly rise to shine!!

You may ask what exactly is life balance, and how can it be balanced? Can we truly have it in life? My answer is, we can have whatever we want, to a degree and usually with conditions attached!! I believe there are 5 dominant practice areas, each required, weighing up in different proportions. These five areas are, our physical health, our social environment, our spiritual growth, our mental capacity, and our emotional stability. Depending on where we are in life: some areas of practice may be required more than others; some more consistently; some occasionally; some methodically; and some in moderation, at differing times, and within various challenges. These five areas are important for our balance.

Physical – We need this area of balance because mobility and exercise is one of the most important things you can do to improve your health. It reduces ill health and increases our chances of longer life. By going to the gym, being more physically minded, or using what we have around the house (if you're not a gym type of person), such as DVD exercises, household items for weights, etc., but most importantly, enjoy it!

Social – Balance in this area gives a sense of stability of life, such as getting time with friends, enjoying yourself, and finding time for *you*. Perhaps build more of a social life into your routine. So very often, when we are busy, this is one of the first things to be dropped. By recognising its importance, it may bring it more up the priority ladder.
Have a social outlet that focuses on you. I created having a *JOY* day; why don't you have one?   spend a day, *Just On Yourself.*

Spiritual – This is a balance area that is unique to each of us. Transpersonal theories focus on research that says a spiritual outlook that is beyond the immediate, leads to a goodness in us that promotes a healthier and happier person. Spiritual thinking refers to the deeper parts of you that lets you make meaning of your world. According to research ignoring this side of your balance can actually deprive you of a more fulfilled life.

For me, my belief in God of the Holy Bible helps me to focus on more spiritual things, such as whether I am growing and being more fulfilled in the area of my knowledge and understanding of my faith.

Mental – This balance supports mental capacity to cope in life. Water and nutrition is also a good mental stimulant. It is also good to surround yourself with positive people, and with peace, meditation, and prayer, as well as sometimes just having a sense of stillness. Talk through your feelings; don't keep them bottled up. Mental health can change, depending on circumstances, and has a strong correlation to psychological wellbeing.

Developing my interests, learning and building my skills, stretching my mental capacity, reading, and broadening my horizons are all things that help me with my wellbeing.

Emotional – We need this balance, and it is sometimes defined as having a relaxed body, and an open heart and mind. It has links to self-esteem and feeling safe and secure with emotions and feelings. Being *in the now* helps too, and not in the past or future, of which we can do nothing about. Watch your thoughts and feelings: are you happy, or sad or negative? Are you dealing with it? Is it reducing or getting bigger? Emotional checks are so important to be aware of for all round health. You need to see it is important to recognise when you are out of balance with one or the other, not having a true acknowledgment of what is important, and the impact it can have on your body and the fulfilment you can get from it. You also need to value time, or give enough energy to a specific area of allowing—allowing the ease of flow in your life to reflect the wants and needs you have, to become more fulfilled to know which area of balance is needed and when.

So how are you doing in these five balance areas? Remember where your mind goes, your energy flows. Are you in need of more of one area of balance on one day than another? On what basis do you make this decision? Is it a healthy balance of self-care and self-love, and a desire to work towards a healthy life balance? Do you need a healthy balance between them all right now, and if so, how? Do you have a way to plan them into your day, week, month, or year? Dynamic Heights has a colour coded template planner that can be ordered for free, to use if you think this will be of help. Check out the online resources at the end of this book for further information.

With growing self-belief, and an increased desire to change, as well as limiting our negativity, stepping out of our comfort zone, and having passion and enthusiasm, with motivation towards a confident action, then you can do anything!! Quite literally, anything!!!

I believe I can assist you in drawing out your indomitable strength through my programmes, by using **Dynamic Heights' A–F principle.**

Application of action – to do anything in life takes application and action, with a mind of attention, with the least distractions.

Boldness to take it on – is a way of going for something that will benefit you and your purpose, whether in speech or **application**; being bold with respect to self and others is vital, and shouldn't be applied without it.

Commitment to a decision – When you are committed to something, you usually want to follow it through. Be **committed** to be **bold** in your **application** of life change. Commitment takes consistent action, and releases a power that drives you on, which is usually described as motivation.

Diligent and methodical – Being diligent is about meticulously not giving up, and having focused attention on your **application**. There is usually some element of sacrifice during this time, but it is oh so worth it!! Having a desire will bring diligence; and when you take **action**, it will flow through.

Effort and energy – Effort is action; effort is sacrifice in taking something on and doing it well. Effort is all about **diligent commitment** with a **boldness** of **application.**

Focus – Focus keeps you on track, with a vision and a goal in mind, and working towards it on a daily occurrence. With focus, you gain tenacity to be able to challenge matters of concern, and work through and move on. Focus is what is lacking in many women's lives; a short burst of focus every now and then will allow you to get on and then stay on track.

A-B-C-D-E-F **Applications** that are **bold**, applied with **commitment** and **diligence,** with increased **effort** and a specific **focus,** will keep you operating from a Dynamic Height.

Dynamic Heights Anagrams

OCD – We all have **Options** to choose from, **Choices** to make from those options, and **Decisions** to take from those choices.

AA – **Accountable Actions:** Having people in our life who support us, to stay on board and hold us accountable, is a vital component in our achievements. Accountability holds us to something we may not even be able to do without another listening ear, or a little push or a shoulder to lean on.

CIA – **Credibility, Integrity, and Authenticity:** CIA is an essential component when wanting to develop on a personal level, and stay true to self. These values go a long way in building a genuine character.

CID – **Confidence, Individuality, and Dignity:** These are essential beliefs and ways of living life, good to build on these.

JOY – **Just on Yourself** – We all need time to relax, chill, and rest. We need at least one day in the week or month to spend J.O.Y. This will allow your mind, body, and soul to be replenished, recharged, and more connected to self. Free your mind to be clear, and uninterrupted. What could you spend your joy days on? Walking, listening to music, visiting a friend, going for a coffee, praying, meditating, relaxing, sleeping, resting, watching inspirational videos, or even that movie you never had time for? Get your hair or nails done, or your feet massaged, write that journal, and tidy up your kitchen drawers like you've been meaning to do, forever! Refresh your bedroom, have a nice relaxing bubble bath. Whatever it is, if it is purposeful and intentional, then do it!! Build your JOY into your calendar, and let nothing interrupt it or take its place; value YOU! Give yourself time to recharge. Apply confidence to yourself by giving back to yourself a much-needed treat, full of JOY.

Dynamic Heights Affirmations

"You cannot gain without pain, so it won't be in vain; you just have to sustain."

"When opportunities are a flow, your future will begin to grow."

"Do what you love, love what you do."

"Life is a journey of discovery; get on board to find your true destination."

"Understanding your gift is like discovering a diamond on a beach: once you find it, you will keep it for life." (But remember to take it out and shine it up every now and again.)

"A true blessing comes when you give someone a piece of your gift"

"Confidence can come easy; just be ready to take the steps required to get there!

"Don't take each day for granted; be grateful you have been granted each day."

"Your life can mirror your thoughts and your thoughts can become your life."

"Look beyond the stars, there is a galaxy of experiences beyond them."

"Dynamic Woman of Worth, you are so worth it."

Be confident in your own abilities, no-one else can be you, or do what you do.

"Time is precious; it is a gift you can invest in it or waste it—it's your choice now you choose".

Other affirmations I have come across that I like:

"Sunshine always comes after rain." – Anonymous

"You'll never become who you are meant to become by remaining who you are." – JoAnna Brandi

"The bad news is time flies; the good news is you're the pilot." – Michael Altshuler

"You'll never leave where you are until you decide where you'd rather be." – Anonymous

"Some succeed because they are destined to, but most succeed because they are determined to." – Henry Van Dyke

"Don't count the days; make the days count."
– Muhammad Ali

"Your life does not get better by chance; it gets better by change." – Jim Rohn

"Your life moves in the direction of your most dominant thoughts." – Anonymous

"You can't discover new oceans unless you have the courage to lose sight of the shore."
– Anonymous

Confidence comes not from always being right, but from not fearing to be wrong."
– Peter T. McIntyre

Conclusion – Next Steps

So, you now have all the tools to know *How to Be a Confident Woman in 7 Easy Steps.*

If this book has resonated with you, then there are some actions you can take right now:

Opportunity to developing your journey with Dynamic Heights

- Put the principles and the strategies from this book into practice

- Write a review on Amazon regarding this book. (Supporting each other as women is key)

- Contact me if you require coaching one-to-one or interested in a training course

- Join the accountable members club

- Follow me on social media

- Book a speaking engagement on confidence for your organisation

- Visit www.confidentwomanin7steps.com for free gifts and information on workshops and online courses. www.dynamicheights.com

- Share your insights and progress that you're making with others in your life

- Buy a copy of this book for your friend; if you benefited, share the love!

- STAY TRUE TO YOUR SELF, and RISE in order TO SHINE !!

Dynamic Heights Women of Worth Training Programme

This training programme is a personal development, motivational, self-empowerment training course, allowing you to explore, contemplate, and discover who you are and whom you can become. It is an opportunity to tap into your hidden areas of desire, which you put a lid on and hardly expose to light. When we have a passion to do something different, to use our talents and skills, but do nothing substantial with it, it can be debilitating. This dynamic training programme allows you to confidently open the box, look inside, and see for yourself your true potential, and your ability to transform your thoughts into real action, whether it be a new career, a new business, or a new personality. Whatever it is, this is a transformational and dynamic programme, where you meet like-minded women who really want to get on in life but have not had the full drive or commitment to do so. Coming soon will be online training resources, tools, tips and programmes, so connect with me if you want to find out more.

One-to-one Coaching – Personal and Professional

The one-to-one coaching service provides you with support in areas of job interviews, personal and professional life coaching, presentation skills, confidence building, personality testing, and business coaching. Alongside of improving your confidence towards lasting changes, the coaching will assist you to achieve your goals through working out your solutions to matters of concern, hence reducing negative impact, and finding clarity through understanding perspectives and forming a clear vision. There will also be support through your areas of growth, to increase your success in moving forward.

Short Courses and Workshops

Dynamic Heights provides a number of training courses, workshops and events created to rejuvenate and recharge you for the next phase of your career and business. It is an opportunity: to reflect on past actions, both good and bad; to confidently prepare for your future; to identify what is challenging; and work through sessions for practical ways to eradicate problems to improve your life, reach new heights, build your potential, and claim your new way forward.

Personality Testing

This testing will allow you to know more about yourself, and also to understand your personality much better. It will also help you to understand how others view you. It has components to gather a deeper and more powerful relationship to your spirituality. It can work towards increasing your success in life by allowing your wisdom and knowledge to accelerate your personal growth in life. Understanding your personality to *know exactly how you tick,* set your clock to operate on your time! At the same time, you can value the clock times of others, metaphorically speaking.

Women who have been coached on this have found it refreshing, but also mind blowing too, as they connect with who they are, without guilt or shame, and acknowledge it and own it, but also understand it. One woman, whom I will never forget, described the revelation of discovering her personality type as "looking into her soul." It allows ongoing understanding during the eight weeks coaching programme, to help shape a new approach to your character and the changes you want to make. Change comes much more naturally as you begin to understand the real stumbling blocks that hold you back, leading to a lighter disposition and a stronger sense of self control particularly when it comes to relationships with others.

Online Membership – Thoughts to Action

Continued support and approaches, similar to the training and coaching programme, but is a good follow up for those who have been on the courses but want that something extra afterwards, and do not want to end the experience of personal steady growth.

Regular support and accountability with other like-minded, switched-on women, who are on a similar journey of a personal and business discovery.

The beauty is that you will get support and encouragement, no matter what stage of your journey you are on, from trusted, committed women, who have your back.

Fuel your passion, and make real time and space to work on your business growth, and personal development, with accountable actions and themed online monthly talks, as well as social media private forums to balance out and connect in between months.

An opportunity to attend a bi-yearly, face-to-face meet-up during a networking, speaking, and motivation event.

A free copy of this book, if you join up as a member.

Coaching discount for any of the one-to-one packages.

An opportunity to grow alongside other women of worth.

Webinars

There will be a series of webinars, sharing motivational topics that will help shape and develop stronger commitments to moving forward and onward. There will also be an opportunity to share more about the Dynamic Heights programmes, and to ask questions and gain further information and insight. These webinars will soon be released for you to register and attend online, allowing you to be engaged, informed, and inspired along the way.

Speaking Engagements

Contact Dynamic Heights for bookings for motivational speaking engagement to talk on confidence to your group, event or organisation. www.dynamicheights.com

Testimonials

Sharing some of the feedback from clients whom Dynamic Heights has worked with:

Hi Mumba, it was wonderful meeting you and fellow participants today. Having experienced today, I cannot wait for the rest of the course. Thank you for the wonderful Women of Worth programme you have for us, and for leading it so beautifully. It definitely lives up to its name: WOW!!!! **Juliet Lapinski – Women of Worth participant**

I met Mumba whilst working together. During this time, Mumba mentioned her skills in coaching and development, when I discussed I had a couple of job interviews coming up. Mumba was amazing in drawing out skills and qualities in myself that I had not considered, and had me 110% prepared for my interview. Mumba's expertise in Interview Coaching gave me the confidence to lead both my interviews, and I was successful in getting offered the position. I highly recommend Mumba for Interview Preparation Coaching—she gets results. **Aneesa Ahmad, Waste Manager at NuGeneration Limited**

I met Mumba at a coaching conference in the midst of a challenging crossroads in my career—one of the reasons I had attended the conference in the first place. We clicked straight away; she has an amiable and dynamic personality, with a natural talent for exploring pertinent issues. I found her friendly and supportive in the way she helped me work towards solutions and goals. It was very effective, and I have greatly appreciated her perspective and skills. I would recommend her to anyone wanting to explore the next step in their lives, whether personal or professional. **Chris Oxborrow**

Mumba has been inspiring, and is such a lovely individual, who has been caring, funny, and helpful. She always had a positive attitude, and was lenient and patient. She has helped open doors for many in self-awareness, and will stay with us. I couldn't have asked for someone with a better personality than her to teach me on this course. **Marya Ahmed**

Mumba delivered outplacement support to one of our teams during a period of restructure. Her calm, focused delivery and empathy enabled people to reflect on the reality of their current situation, and emerge with new approaches and fresh perspectives. Mumba is an experienced personal development trainer and coach who is committed to using her expertise to support people through the practical and emotional challenges of transition. **Margaret Glossip**

I recommend Dynamic Heights Service to anybody who has ever felt lost in life, who could do with that extra bit of support to get back on their feet, and that extra bit of confidence and self-belief to achieve goals and be successful. I consider myself to be successful, and Mumba (Dynamic Heights) was a great support to me throughout my journey to that success, and beyond. **Cassandra Brown – Coaching client and attendee at Balancing your Life with Confidence Workshop**

I approached Mumba for one-to-one coaching because I had many aspects to my freelance work, and I wanted to find a way to bring it all together. Mumba was really effective at drawing out what was really important to me, and helped identify strengths and opportunities I didn't know I had. She helped me to define my business identity. This has helped me to stay focused when opportunities arise. She really cares about her clients, and often gets in touch with me to find out how my work is going. I am happy to recommend Mumba as a coach. **Fiona Gray, Specialist/Instructor for Older Adult Fitness**

Prior to receiving coaching with Mumba, I was nervous about the upcoming interview and had no idea how I would go about answering the questions that may come up. I felt bewildered with the application process and application form. After being coached by Mumba, I was able to deliver a clear and concise application form, and approach the interview with confidence. If you would like to gain a thorough knowledge on how to write an application form, and gain more confidence at an interview, then I would highly recommend Mumba's coaching. **Lorna Young, Centre 4 Success**

My experience of Mumba is that she is a woman of integrity, reliability, commitment, and understanding, and she is excellent at what she provides as a coach. Mumba listens to me attentively, and helps me to think out-of-the-box in order to meet my business aims. Where I have experienced *stumbling blocks,* she has been able to tap into my psyche in order to transform my negative thoughts into positive ones. After a coaching session with Mumba, I am motivated, inspired, and energised, knowing that I will give 100 per cent to making my business work. She has made me even more passionate about Family Mediation on so many levels. I wholeheartedly recommend Mumba, and will continue to work with her, as it is time and money well spent. **Zalika Akinsete, Family Mediator**

**HOW TO BE A CONFIDENT WOMAN
IN 7 EASY STEPS
DISCOVER YOUR GIFT, IGNITE YOUR PASSION,
BUILD YOUR INDOMITABLE SPIRIT
AND
ACHIEVE YOUR AMBITIOUS ASPIRATIONS!**

Printed in Poland
by Amazon Fulfillment
Poland Sp. z o.o., Wrocław